At one time May-day was co
Marian, for it is the day when
Stow tells us how one May
Katharine, with a company of
near Greenwich, when they
dressed in green, led by their captain, who called himself Robin
Hood. He invited the royal company to watch their display of
archery and then, in a flower-decked arbour, deep in the woods,
entertained them to a feast of venison and wine, 'to their great
contentment'.

Also in this series in Panther Books

MARY CATHCART BORER

London
Walks and Legends

PANTHER
Granada Publishing

Panther Books
Granada Publishing Ltd
8 Grafton Street, London W1X 3LA

Published by Panther Books 1981
Reprinted 1983

A Granada Paperback Original
Copyright © Mary Cathcart Borer 1981

ISBN 0-583-13308-8

Printed and bound in Great Britain by
Cox & Wyman Ltd, Reading

Set in Plantin

All rights reserved. No part of this publication may
be reproduced, stored in a retrieval system, or
transmitted, in any form, or by any means, electronic,
mechanical, photocopying, recording or otherwise,
without the prior permission of the publishers.

This book is sold subject to the conditions that it
shall not, by way of trade or otherwise, be lent,
re-sold, hired out or otherwise circulated
without the publisher's prior consent in any
form of binding or cover other than that in
which it is published and without a similar
condition including this condition being imposed
on the subsequent purchaser.

CONTENTS

I should like to thank the Royal Almonry Office, Buckingham Palace, for the information in regard to Royal Maundy Money and the Archivist of Cassell Ltd for giving me the former site of the Belle Sauvage inn.

M C B

INTRODUCTION

London is at least two thousand years old, and many of the legends surrounding the heart of the ancient city belong to the twilight days of remote history, when happenings which could not be explained rationally were attributed to the mysterious forces of good or evil. A number of these beliefs lingered on into the eighteenth century – the Age of Reason – and some even to the present day. After reading this book, I hope you will find an added interest, when you go exploring the places where miracles have happened and ghosts have assuredly appeared.

I have begun the walks at obviously accessible places and none of them involves more walking than you feel inclined to do, for in each case a bus or tube will take you most or all of the way.

M C B

FROM CHARING CROSS TO
THE GUILDHALL

The May-pole in the Strand
Oranges and Lemons, Say the Bells of St Clement's
The Man Who Lost Himself
Fleet Street
King Lud and Ludgate Hill
Bow Bells and the Cockneys
Gog and Magog

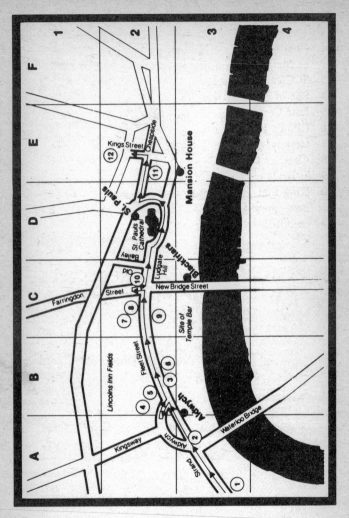

A

A

BUSES
Strand: 1, 6, 9, 11, 13, 15, 77, 77A, 77C, 168, 170, 172, 176.
Fleet Street: 4, 6, 9, 11, 15, 168, 502, 513
Ludgate Hill: 4, 6, 9, 11, 15, 18, 23, 141, 502, 513.
Cheapside: 8, 22, 25, 501.
Moorgate: 11, 21, 43, 76, 133.

This is only a rough guide to the buses and you may need to consult the London Transport Bus Map.

UNDERGROUNDS
Charing Cross
Embankment
Aldwych
St Paul's
Blackfriars
Bank
Temple

THE MAY-POLE IN THE STRAND

From Charing Cross walk down the Strand (1). *At the eastern end, just beyond the point where Aldwych branches off to the left, is James Gibbs' beautiful little church of St Mary-le-Strand* (2) built in the reign of Queen Anne. It is near the site of the medieval St Mary-le-Strand, of which Thomas à Becket was a rector in the twelfth century, and close by was an ancient cross, under which the judges sometimes sat to administer justice outside the City walls. The cross was taken down at the Reformation and a May-pole set up in its place: and here Londoners enjoyed the May-day revels which mankind has celebrated since the days of the sun-worshippers, centuries before the young people of Rome used to spend the day in dancing and singing, in honour of Flora, the goddess of fruit and flowers.

May-day revels took place all over England and there were several May-poles in London, but the May-pole in the Strand, said to be a hundred feet high, was the most famous of them all.

At one time May-day was consecrated to Robin Hood and Maid Marian, for it is the day when Robin is thought to have died. John Stow tells us how one May-day King Henry VIII and Queen Katharine, with a company of courtiers, were riding in the woods near Greenwich, when they came upon a band of tall yeomen, dressed in green, led by their captain, who called himself Robin Hood. He invited the royal company to watch their display of archery and then, in a flower-decked arbour, deep in the woods, entertained them to a feast of venison and wine, 'to their great contentment'.

By this time, in nearly every village throughout the country and every parish in London, a May-pole, decorated with ribbons and flowers, was set up, a May-queen was chosen and the day passed in archery, morris-dancing and revelry, while as evening fell large bonfires were lighted, round which people danced and feasted or watched a play. In the Strand, young people usually ended the day at the 'Cock and Pie', a tavern which stood in the Via de Aldewych, which was later to become Drury Lane.

St Mary-le-Strand.
British Tourist Authority

But in London 1517 was Evil May-day, when the revelry changed to rioting amongst the apprentices, in protest at the ever increasing number of foreigners who were flocking into the City. The trouble broke out round the May-pole which was set up each day in the middle of Leadenhall Street, in front of the south door of Stow's church of St Andrew – which is why it is called St Andrew Undershaft – and it quickly spread. It was

16

another three weeks before it was suppressed, during which time untold damage was done: and after that May-day celebrations were never the same. The St Andrew May-pole had been left lying in Shaft Alley, and when the curate of St Katherine Cree, preaching at St Paul's Cross, denounced it as an idol, it was cut up and burned, while during the Commonwealth May-poles were altogether forbidden, as 'the last remnants of vile heathenism', it being asserted that people were quite ignorant of their 'original intent and meaning'.

The May-poles all disappeared: and by this time the old church of St Mary-le-Strand had also gone, having been pulled down by Protector Somerset when he built the first Somerset House. But with the Restoration, a new May-pole was set up here in the Strand, 'far more glorious, bigger and higher than ever', to the delight of King Charles and the Duke of York, while 'the little children did much rejoice, and ancient people did clap their hands, saying golden days began to appear'.

It was paid for by John Clarges, a blacksmith living close by, whose daughter eventually rose in the social scale and married General Monck, the Duke of Albemarle – although there were those who said that her first husband was still alive. To the accompaniment of trumpets and drums and joyful cheering, the new May-pole was placed in position and the revelries were opened by a party of morris-dancers, 'finely decked with purple scarfs, in their half-shirts, with a pipe and tabor, the ancient music', who danced round it. There it stood for the next fifty years, by which time it had become decayed and dangerous, and much reduced in height by wind and rain.

In 1713 a third May-pole was set up close by, opposite Somerset House. After this, however, the junketings were never so abandoned. It stood for only five years, and then it was bought from the parishioners by Sir Isaac Newton, who sent it to Wanstead Park, where it was used to support a large telescope, 125 feet long, said at the time to be the biggest in Europe.

By this time James Gibbs' new church of St Mary-le-Strand had been built, and it was here, in 1750, that Charles Edward Stuart, the Young Pretender, on a secret visit to London, when he stayed with Lady Primrose in nearby Essex Street, is thought to have been received into the Church of England, having formally renounced his Catholic faith in order to further the cause of the Jacobites.

It was about this time that May-day festivals in the Strand became associated with milkmaids. In 1771, J T Smith, in his *Book For A Rainy Day*, recalled the May-day celebrations of his boyhood, when milkmaids danced round an obelisk laden with valuable plate hired from the silversmiths. 'The most showy flowers of the season were arranged so as to fill up the openings between the dishes, plates, butterboats, cream-jugs and tankards. This obelisk was carried by two children in gold-laced hats, six or more handsome milkmaids in pink and blue gowns. . . yellow or scarlet petticoats, neatly quilted, high-heeled shoes, mob-caps with lappets of lace resting on their shoulders; nosegays on their bosoms and flat Woffington hats covered with ribbons of every colour. . . A smart, slender fellow of a fiddler, commonly wearing a sky-blue coat, with a hat profusely covered with ribbons, attended; and the master of the group was accompanied by a constable to protect the plate from too close a pressure of the crowd, when the maids danced before the doors of his customers.'

The London chimney-sweeps were soon to have a holiday of their own on May-day, which is said to have first been held when Mrs Elizabeth Montagu – the wealthiest of the Blue-Stockings – began, late in the eighteenth century, to give them a May-day dinner of roast beef and plum pudding in the grounds of her house in Portman Square. She gave it, she said, 'so that they might enjoy one happy day in the year', and in gratitude for the recovery of her nephew, the eccentric son of Lady Mary Wortley Montagu, who ran away from Westminster school and became a chimney sweep for a few weeks, until he was discovered and returned to his family.

ORANGES AND LEMONS, SAY THE BELLS OF ST CLEMENT'S

Only a few yards east of St Mary-le-Strand, near the Law Courts (5), is the church of St Clement Danes (3). There has been a church

18

on this site for a thousand years, ever since King Alfred granted the land, an uninhabited stretch of waste, between Ludgate and Westminster, to a small colony of Danes who had married English wives. Here they built their first little chapel, dedicated to St Clement, the patron saint of sailors, who had been canonized after 100 AD when, during the Christian persecutions, the Romans had tossed him into the sea, weighted by an anchor.

Harold Harefoot, son of Canute, was buried in the church-yard of St Clement. After the brief three years of his reign, during which he undid most of the good his father had achieved, he was first buried at Westminster, but when his half-brother, Harthacanute, succeeded him, though to no better effect, he ordered Harold's body to be taken from its tomb and thrown into the river, to avenge an old insult to his mother. The body drifted ashore and was retrieved by a fisherman, who gave the unworthy Harold a decent burial at St Clement Danes.

The old church survived the Great Fire, but by then it was in a sad state of decay. In 1680 it was taken down and a new church built by Edward Pierce, under the direction of Sir Christopher Wren. The tower and steeple were added early in the reign of George I, and the tower had an exceptionally beautiful peal of bells, which played the Old Hundredth Psalm and other melodies, three times a day, at nine o'clock in the morning, at midday and at five o'clock.

By this time Clare market (4), established by the Earl of Clare in 1657, close by in Clement's Inn Fields, between Drury Lane and Lincoln's Inn Fields, was the important source of supply for the people living in the narrow streets and alleys which had grown up here. Amongst the produce they bought were oranges and lemons, which were landed by barge below London Bridge, at the dock where the Spanish fruit arrived, and carried by porters to the Strand, through the churchyard and into the market.

'Oranges and lemons, say the bells of St Clement's', but when the nursery rhyme was written, no one knows. It is quoted in *Tommy Thumb's Pretty Song Book*, which was published about 1744, but there is an earlier version in

Wynkyn de Worde's *Demaundes Joyous*, a nursery book which appeared early in the sixteenth century, nearly a hundred years before Clare market was established. This gives support to the claim that the jingle was referring to the church of St Clement, Eastcheap, which was closer to the river and the fruit dock. Yet the tradition that it belongs to St Clement Danes is very strong, and when the old Clement's Inn, about which Justice Shallow and Falstaff had so much to say, was in its heyday, the porter would visit every tenant on the first of

St Clement Danes.
British Tourist Authority

January each year and present him with an orange and a lemon, expecting in return a tip of half a crown.

St Clement Danes was grievously damaged during the bombing of World War Two, and except for the Sanctus bell, high up in the belfry, the bells were all cracked when they fell to the ground, but the church has been beautifully restored and the bells recast, so that once more they ring out the old tunes.

Today, the church where Dr Johnson regularly worshipped, in a pew in the north gallery, is the church of the Royal Air Force, honouring the memory of the thousands of men and women of the British and Commonwealth air forces who lost their lives during the Second World War, and also of the 9,000 members of the United States Air Force, who died while serving in Britain.

THE MAN WHO LOST HIMSELF

Before the Law Courts (**5**) were built, in 1874, and Kingsway, in 1900, a tangle of sordid little winding passages and over-crowded courts had developed between Lincoln's Inn Fields and the Strand, which all had to be cleared away.

So bad had conditions become here, that there is a sad little story of a young man from the country, carrying a black bag, who set off one night from Portugal Street to reach the Strand, but never did find his way, returning forlornly over and over again, to his starting point, each time looking more tired and dispirited. Days became weeks. On foggy nights his wraith-like figure was to be seen, groping its way in dismal frustration through Clare market (**4**). The weeks became months and his unhappy ghost was sometimes seen, still carrying the black bag, trying to find its way through the maze. Then he just faded away. He never reached the Strand and no one ever heard of him again.

FLEET STREET

Just to the east of St Clement Danes stood the stocks, which were not taken down until 1820, and walking past the spot, a few yards on, where Temple Bar once stood, we come to the boundary of the City of London and the beginning of Fleet Street, where every foot of the way has a story to tell, beginning with Number One, Child's Bank (**6**), which was established in 1671, at the sign of the Marygold, where once had been a tavern. Until this time, the pawnbrokers and goldsmiths of London had acted as bankers, but Child's was the first house to concentrate entirely on banking.

This was Telson's bank, in Charles Dickens' *A Tale of Two Cities*, and its early customers included Charles II, Prince Rupert, Nell Gwyn, Pepys, Dryden and the Duke and Duchess of Marlborough. The story goes that in 1689, when there was a rumour that the bank was in difficulties, Sarah Churchill called for her coach and made a gallant dash round the town, visiting all her friends, collecting as much gold as she could, and driving down to the bank just in time, as the run was starting, to enable the cashier to meet all the demands and restore confidence.

There is another story that on a dark winter's night, during the French Revolution, the bank had a midnight visitor. It was the Marquise de Rambouillet, who left two large chests at the bank for safe-keeping, departed again for France and was never heard of again. When at last the chests were opened, it was found that one contained nothing but a store of decaying foodstuff, but in the other was gold plate and diamonds worth £100,000.

It was from this point in Fleet Street, by Temple Bar, that Dr Johnson once said he liked sometimes to stand and examine the faces of the passers by, declaring that between eleven and four o'clock every sixth man was an author. 'In the afternoon, when they have all dined, or composed themselves to pass the day without a dinner, their passions have full play, and I can perceive one man wondering at the stupidity of the public, by which his new book has been totally neglected; another cursing the French, who fright away literary curiosity by their threat of invasion; another swearing at his bookseller, who will advance no money without "copy"; another perusing his publisher's bill; another murmuring at an unanswerable criticism; another

22

determined to write no more to a generation of barbarians; and another wishing to try once again whether he cannot awaken the drowsy world to a sense of his merit.'

Fleet Street is full of memories. *Down on the left, alongside Number 166, is the entrance to Johnson's Court, leading to Dr Johnson's house in Gough Square (7),* a delightful late seventeenth-century house, where he lived from 1748-1759 and wrote his Dictionary.

A few yards farther east is the Cheshire Cheese (8), which was built after the Great Fire, although its vaults are far older. One of its many claims to fame is the tradition of its wonderful beef-steak pudding, which was served every Saturday throughout the winter months. It weighed anything from fifty to eighty pounds and consisted of a suet crust in a huge basin into which was piled 'beef-steaks, kidneys, oysters, larks, mushrooms, and wonderous spices and gravies, the secret of which was only known to the compounder'. It took sixteen to twenty hours to boil and it was claimed that on a windy day the smell of it had been known to reach as far as the Stock Exchange.

On the opposite side of the street stands St Bride's church (9), which is thought to have been built on the site of the first Christian worship in England, for Roman remains have been found in the crypt. The first two churches were destroyed, probably by fire, and it was the third St Bride's which became one of the City churches from which the curfew was rung. Wynkyn de Worde, Caxton's apprentice, set up his printing press next door and was buried in the old church. But the St Bride's you see today, with its 'wedding cake' spire, was the work of Christopher Wren after the Great Fire. It has been restored after the bomb damage of World War Two.

Fleet Street ends at Ludgate Circus. To the north runs Farringdon Street, to the south New Bridge Street, both covering the old Fleet river, which now runs in a culvert twenty feet below ground, draining into the Thames by Blackfriars Bridge.

KING LUD AND LUDGATE HILL

A few yards down Farringdon Street, on the east side, once stood the terrible Fleet prison, the worst of all the debtors' prisons, and on the corner of the hill is the King Lud tavern (**10**), named after the legendary Celtic king of Britain, who was said to have built the gate and been buried beneath it. The Lud Gate, which remained until 1760, ran across the hill, about half way up, just to the west of the Wren church of St Martin-Within-Ludgate. This was rebuilt after the Great Fire and part of the City wall is incorporated in the western part of the church. But the purists will tell you that the Lud Gate was not named after King Lud after all, but was originally the Flood or Fleet Gate.

On the left-hand side of the hill, about thirty yards up from the railway bridge, once stood the Belle Sauvage, one of the most splendid of London's coaching inns. In its early days it was known as the Bell on the Hoop, but during the reign of Queen Elizabeth I it came into the possession of Isabel Savage and was known as the Bell Savage. Plays were performed in its courtyard and one of the favourite comic actors was the flat-nosed, squint-eyed little Tarleton, believed to be the original of Hamlet's 'poor Yorick'. The galleried inn was built round three sides of the inner of two courtyards, the outer courtyard, in which a few houses were built, opening on to the north side of the hill: and it is said that it was in one of these houses that John Evelyn first saw and admired the wood carving of the young Grinling Gibbons and recommended his work to King Charles II.

The Bell Savage, which lasted until 1873, advertised forty rooms, good cellarage and stabling for a hundred horses. How it came to be called La Belle Sauvage is not certain, but one story is that early in the seventeenth century, when John Rolph brought to England his frail little bride, the Red Indian princess Pocahontas, who had risked her life to help the first English settlers in Virginia, they had stayed at the inn for a time: and after her death at Gravesend, a few months later, when she was still only twenty-one, the name was changed to the Belle Sauvage, as a salute to her beauty and gallantry.

Branching northwards from Ludgate Hill is the street called Old Bailey – probably part of the ballium or city wall between Ludgate and Newgate – and here the Central Criminal Court now stands, built on the site of the old Newgate prison.

24

BOW BELLS AND THE COCKNEYS

From the top of Ludgate Hill, walk around the north side of St Paul's precinct into Cheapside, passing on your left Foster Lane, Gutter Lane, Wood Street and Milk Street. At this point, cross over Cheapside to the church of St Mary-le-Bow (11), more usually known as Bow Church, which stands nearly in the centre of the square mile of the City.

There has been a church on this site since Norman times and it was once under the direct jurisdiction of the Archbishop of Canterbury. For centuries, until the Great Fire, the highest ecclesiastical court – the Court of Arches – met here, but today it meets at Church House, Westminster.

Why it is called Bow Church is not certain. The original church – St Maria-de-Arcubus or Bow – had a lantern on top of the tower, which was held by four slender, curving stone supports forming arches, but the more likely explanation is that the name is derived from the magnificent Norman arches of the crypt, twenty feet below the present pavement, for this is said to have been the first London church built on arches or 'bows' of stone.

This is one of the churches from which the nine o'clock curfew was rung, warning the prentices that it was time for them to be indoors and for people to put out their lights and go to bed.

Stow says that the bell was usually rung late and the apprentices would sing out:

> 'Clarke of the Bow bell, with the yellow lockes,
> For thy late ringing, thy head shall have knockes'

to which the clerk replied:

> 'Children of Chepe, hold you all still,
> For you shall have Bow bell rung at your will.'

The church had also a beautiful peal of bells – the same that Dick Whittington heard from Highgate Hill and which called him back to London. But the old church was destroyed during the Great Fire, and the present church, with a new peal of bells, was built by Wren. The body of his church was gutted during the bombing of World War Two, but has been restored by Laurence King. Wren's tower and steeple survived, however, and in the new peal of Bow bells, first heard in 1961, are incorporated parts of the seventeenth-century bells.

The legend persists that true cockneys are those who have been born within sound of Bow bells, but there is also a legend about the origin of the word 'cockney'. Today it means someone speaking with a cockney accent who, having been born and bred in the City, knows nothing of country life and ways. However, a 'cockerney' or cockney originally meant someone who had been pampered by the comforts of city life, knowing nothing of the rigours and harshness of country labours. The word may even have been derived from the thirteenth-century French poem *The Land of Cocagne*, where the houses were made of barley sugar and cake, the streets were paved with pastry and the shopkeepers never asked to be paid for their wares, for at this time the French regarded the English as 'cocagnes' or 'beef and pudding men', who indulged themselves in gay living, good eating and hard drinking. And in Tudor times, during the Christmas festivities of the young law students of Lincoln's Inn, their master of the revels, chosen from among their members, was known as the King of the Cocknies.

GOG AND MAGOG

Cross back to the north side of Cheapside, and after Milk Street you come to the short King Street, at the end of which stands London's Guildhall (12), much damaged and altered since it was rebuilt in the early fifteenth century, but beautifully restored and maintained.

Cross the courtyard and pass through the ancient porch into the main chamber of the building, the Great Hall. Here, perched high up on either side of the gallery at the western end, the giants Gog and Magog gaze down inscrutably on all the assemblies, both solemn and festive, which gather below. They are strange, stocky figures, distinctly short in the leg, but splendidly gilded and glittering, looking vaguely Greek, in

Statue of 'Gog' at The Guildhall.
British Tourist Authority

Statue of 'Magog' at The Guildhall.
British Tourist Authority

their helmets and kilts, Gog with his spiked ball and chain, known as a morning star, and Magog with his shield and long spear. They seem aloof and rather puzzled, but they stand to defend the honour of 'this their city, which excels all others as much as these huge giants exceed in stature the common bulk of mankind'.

According to William Caxton, in his *Chronicles of England*, they lived in the days of an Emperor Diocletian, who, some three thousand years ago, ruled over an unspecified part of eastern Europe. Diocletian was blessed with no less than thirty-three difficult and intractable daughters. The Emperor managed to find husbands for them all, but the girls had no interest in matrimony, and in order to regain their lost freedom they arranged together that each should cut her husband's throat. Their outraged father was 'hugely wroth' and planned to put them all to death, but was persuaded instead to pack them all into a small boat, with six months' supply of food, and set them adrift. They survived and eventually reached the shores of Britain, 'an island that was all wilderness', which they named Albion, after the eldest of the perfidious sisters.

Soon, however, they began to crave for the diversion of men's company, and the Devil now began his serious work of retribution, for he created thirty-three demon husbands for them, so that the young women, in due course, gave birth to a brood of horrible giants, who rampaged over southern Britain, to the terror of the native Celts.

The giants flourished in Britain and had things all their own way, until the Greeks sacked Troy, about 1200 BC, and the Trojans were put to flight. Then one of their most enterprising soldiers, Brutus, reaching farther than the others, pressed westwards through the Mediterranean, set on a course of exploration and conquest. He reached France, and with the help of the Gauls, invaded southern Britain.

Albion's fierce giant of a son, who was also called Albion, rallied his cousins to do battle with the invaders, arming themselves with battle axes and their murderous looking 'morning stars'. When the astonished Trojans were confronted with these men of gigantic stature and vast strength, they were at first soundly beaten, and Brutus ordered a tactical retreat, but he was not to be thwarted.

At dead of night, he ordered his men to dig a long, deep trench, into the bottom of which they planted sharp, pointed stakes. They hid the trench beneath piles of dead leaves, and as dawn broke they fired a shower of arrows and darts from behind it into the giants' camp. The enraged giants were stung into making a fresh attack on the Trojans, but as they rushed forward their leaders fell headlong into the hidden trench and were impaled on the stakes. The rest fled in terror and Brutus and his men chased after them into the west country, reaching as far as Devon.

One version of the next part of the story is that Albion was killed and the fight went on until only two giants, Gog and Magog, survived. They were taken prisoner and Brutus and his men then turned eastwards again, until they reached the Thames. They followed its course downstream and on the first rising ground above the estuary, where London stands today, they founded their first settlement, which they called Troynovant or New Troy. Brutus built his palace, where the Guildhall now stands, and Gog and Magog were chained to its gate as doorkeepers.

This account, in *The History of the Trojan Wars and Troy's Destruction*, was published by Sarah Bates in 1735, at the sign of the Sun and Bible, in Giltspur Street, but a few years later another version of the story appeared, in which it was said that the only survivor of the giants was Gogmagog, who was eighteen feet tall – some say twenty-five – and that the giant we call Gog was really Corineus, a younger brother of Brutus, who offered to engage Gogmagog in a final combat.

'Gogmagog presently grasped Corineus with all his might, broke three of his ribs, two on his right side and one on his left. At which Corineus, highly enraged, roused up his whole strength, and snatching him upon his shoulders, ran with him as fast as he was able for the weight, to the next shore, and there, getting upon the top of a high rock, hurled down the savage monster into the sea; where, falling by the side of craggy rocks, he was cruelly torn to pieces and coloured the waves with his blood.' And the place where he fell, near Plymouth, was ever afterwards called the Giant's Leap.

Yet Corineus was no giant, and it is as Gog and Magog that the two Guildhall giants have survived, coming down from the gallery into the hall each day for their dinner, so they say, as they hear St Paul's clock strike twelve, although no one has ever yet seen them do it.

Their effigies have been in the Guildhall for more than five hundred years. They were frail things of wicker and plaster in the early days, and were carried in the processions of the midsummer festivals, just as, to the delight of the onlookers, wicker giants were carried elsewhere in Britain and in many parts of Europe, on festive occasions.

A writer of the sixteenth century tells of 'midsummer pageants in London, where to make the people wonder, are set forth great and uglie giants marching as if they were alive, and armed at all points, but within they are stuffed full of brown paper and tow, which the shrewd boys, underpeering, do guilefully discover, and turne to greate derision'.

In France, after being promenaded through the streets for several days, the giants were sometimes burned. The practice continued into the eighteenth century, a strange survival of the grim custom of the Celts of ancient Gaul, as recorded by Roman explorers. The Druid priests would preserve condemned criminals in order that they should be sacrificed to the gods, at a solemn festival which took place every five years. When the time came, an enormous cage of wickerwork or wood and grass was built, into which the wretched criminals were herded, together with cattle and other animals, and in it they were burnt alive, in order to bring fertility to the earth.

However, Gog and Magog were never burned, but always returned to their stations, which at one time were on either side of the door of the Council Chamber.

They survived the Great Fire, but they were getting very dilapidated, and during the reign of Queen Anne new, more durable giants were made, this time of carved wood. During the last war they were lost in the bombing, but now they are back again, carved in limewood, to remind us of the day when Britain was peopled by the giants. Some of them may have reached as far into the country as the Gogmagog hills, just south-east of Cambridge, but these hills are named after another branch of the family. This Gogmagog fell in love with the nymph Granta, and when she would have nothing to do with him, the disconsolate giant turned himself into Gogmagog, the larger of the two hills.

FROM LUDGATE CIRCUS TO CLERKENWELL

Rahere and St Bartholomew's Hospital

Visions at the Charterhouse

The Knights of St John

Sally in our Alley

Scratching Fanny of Cock Lane

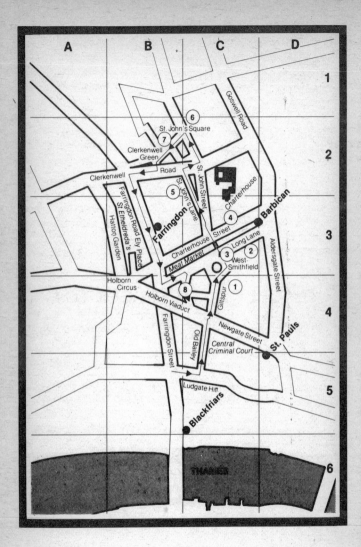

B

B

BUSES
Ludgate Hill: 4, 6, 9, 11, 15, 18, 23, 141, 502, 513.
Holborn Viaduct and Newgate Street: 8, 22, 25, 501.
Smithfield: 277, 279.
John Street: 277, 279.
Clerkenwell Road: 5, 55, 243, 277.

This is only a rough guide to the buses and you may need to consult the London Transport Bus Map.

UNDERGROUNDS
Blackfriars
St Paul's
Farringdon
Barbican

RAHERE AND ST BARTHOLOMEW'S HOSPITAL

From Ludgate Circus walk up Ludgate Hill and turn along Old Bailey. The Central Criminal Court – the 'Old Bailey' – is on your right, on the corner of Newgate Street, and St Sepulchre's Church just opposite, at the corner of Holborn Viaduct and Giltspur Street. Cross over Newgate Street and continue northwards along Giltspur Street, passing on your left Cock Lane (8) (see legend on page 50). You will find yourself in West Smithfield, with St Bartholomew's Hospital (1) on the south-east side and the entrance to Rahere's ancient Church of St Bartholomew (2) on the east side.

Rahere lived more than eight hundred years ago. As a young man he attended the court of Henry I and the first account of him in these early years is far from flattering.

'He drew to friendship with himself those whom he had soothed with his jokes and flatterings. And not content with this, he approached the king's palace with some frequency, and resorted to the tumults of the tumultuous court, and with jocular flattery desired to attract himself with ease the hearts of many. There he made it his business all day long to attend spectacles, banquets and jests, and the rest of the trifles of the court; and with shameless face, betaking himself to the suite now of the king, now of the nobles, he assiduously employed the complaisance that should please them, and obtained with greater ease anything that it pleased him to ask.'

This somewhat sour description comes from a manuscript in the Cottonian collection, written late in the twelfth century, not long after Rahere's death, by a prior who must have known him, but there is no evidence here that he ever became the King's minstrel or jester, as is so often said, or was anything but one of the gayest members of the Court.

In 1120 the White Ship, which had set sail from Normandy without the blessing of the priest, sank when it struck a rock in the mouth of the harbour, and the King lost his only son, Prince William, to whom he had been devoted. When the news reached King Henry it is said that he fell unconscious to the ground, and rose never to smile again.

The Court was plunged into a long-lasting mourning and Rahere was saddened and sobered by the tragedy. It was

Entrance to Rahere's ancient Church of St Bartholomew-The-Great.
Marianne Taylor

about this time that he underwent a religious conversion. He
may have been influenced by the goodness and humility of
Queen Matilda, who had died two years earlier, and there is
some evidence, although not wholly convincing, that he had

already become a Prebendary of St Paul's Cathedral, for this was a time of great religious revival in England.

It was soon after the death of the Prince that Rahere decided to undertake a pilgrimage to Rome. He made the long and hazardous journey with no mishap, but on the way home he fell desperately ill with malaria. On his sick bed he vowed that if he recovered and God allowed him to reach England again, he would build a hospital for the poor and, as far as he could, administer to their needs himself. His health returned and he

St Bartholomew-The-Great.
British Tourist Authority

continued his homeward journey, but one night he had a terrifying dream. He was seized by a great creature with the talons and wings of an enormous eagle, which bore him to the top of a high cliff and then dropped him on to a narrow ledge of rock. And as Rahere looked down, he found that he was tottering on the brink of a bottomless pit. He cried out in dreadful terror, and at that moment the creature disappeared. In its place appeared a man of majestic beauty. 'I am Bartholomew, the Apostle of Jesus Christ', said the vision, 'and I have come to help you. I, by the will and command of all the High Trinity. . . have chosen a spot in a suburb of London, at Smithfield, where in my name, thou shalt found a hospital and a church that shall be the House of God. The means will be given to you.'

Rahere awoke from his dream and reached London again. He told his friends what had happened. He must build a church and a hospital, but he came from a poor family and had few resources. His friends advised him to consult the King, who listened sympathetically and, after consulting with the Bishop of London, granted Rahere the site he needed – the eastern part of the Smooth Field, which was just outside the City of London's northern wall but within its jurisdiction. It was a dreary, swampy place, but the land included a stretch known as the King's Market, where every Friday a horse fair was held. By being given this land, Rahere was also entitled to the market tolls, which gave him the means to make his plans. He invited two other divines to help him in his work, Alfune, who had just built the church of St Giles, Cripplegate, and Hagno, an Augustinian.

In 1123 the building of the Augustinian Priory church and the little adjoining hospital was begun and four years later they were completed and dedicated to St Bartholomew, the apostle who is said to have preached the gospel in India and been flayed alive by those who opposed his teaching.

For the next sixteen years, until his death in 1143, when he left a band of thirteen monks at the priory, Rahere was the prior of the monastery church. During these years many miracles of healing took place, both in the church and the hospital, as recorded in the *Book of the Foundation*, a

The North Ambulatory of St Bartholomew-The-Great, founded 1123.
By kind permission of the Rector, The Priory Church of St Bartholomew-The-Great

contemporary record which is now in the British Museum: and they continued during the time of Rahere's successor, Prior Thomas, many more taking place in the church than the hospital, much to the vexation of the hospital for a time.

Each year on St Bartholomew's Day, August 24th, the sick and suffering would be brought to the church and laid before the altar in the little chapel at the east end of the north wall of the church.

Among the long list of miracles we read that on St Bartholomew's Day 'the canones were chanting the second vespers' and 'when they came to the hymn of Mary, the most Blessed Mother of God, at the incensing of the altars', a girl – deaf, dumb and blind – was miraculously cured. And 'on a certain day after compline, the bridle of the tongue of a dumb youth was loosed'. A woman was carried in a litter to the church and 'on the vigil of the festival of the most blessed apostle Bartholomew, about the hour of compline, she began to recover her lost strength'.

Five years after Rahere's death, the *Book of the Foundation* records how the crowds came to the church to be healed on St Bartholomew's Day. 'Sick men oppressed with divers diseases lay prostrate in the Church, while the lamps glowed redly on all sides, beseeching the divine clemency and praying for the presence of the blessed Bartholomew. Nor assuredly was the mercy of God far from them, who is always present at the prayer of those that devotedly ask him.

'For one man rejoices with a cry of jubilation that he has received remedy of his aching head, another, restoration of his walking powers. Here a man rejoices free from ringing in the ears, there one from ulceration of the limbs; here one who has lost soreness of his eyes and received clearness of sight; many rejoice that they were soothed from the distress of fevers, and thundered praises to the honour and glory of the apostle.'

The Priory became a place of pilgrimage, particularly during the days of the church festivals. On these occasions, hucksters and chapmen always appeared, to serve the pilgrims, for pilgrimages were usually regarded as something of a holiday as well as a religious duty, and within a few years the King had granted the Priory a charter for the three days of St Bartholomew's fair, which was first held within the Priory grounds and brought more money for the church and hospital. It soon became an important trade fair, dealing at first mainly in cloth, the merchants keeping their wares inside the Priory

Tomb of Rahere, the founder of St Bartholomew-The-Great.
By kind permission of the Rector, The Priory Church of St Bartholomew-The-Great

walls at night for safety. With the increased tolls the Priory was able to extend its work for the poor and sick. St Bartholomew had kept his promise and for many years to come the Priors of St Bartholomew were the Lords of the Fair.

In the rest of the Smooth Field, which was to become known as Smithfield, the weekly horse market was still held, and on other days of the week it became a place for tournaments and archery contests, some of the tournaments being magnificently staged, especially during the reign of Edward III, who arranged them to entertain his illustrious captives, the kings of France and Scotland. On one occasion, towards the end of his reign, when he was deeply in love with his beautiful mistress, Alice Pierce, he conferred on her the title of 'Lady of the Sun', and taking her hand, led her from the royal apartments in the Tower of London to take her place beside him, in a triumphal chariot, for the drive to Smithfield; and following them was a procession of ladies of the Court, each mounted on a beautiful palfrey, led by a mounted knight.

But the grandest Smithfield tournament on record was held during the reign of Richard II. Invitations were sent to all the courts of Europe. 'At three o'clock on the Sunday after Michaelmas-day, the ceremony began. Sixty horses in rich trappings, each mounted by an esquire of honour, were seen advancing in a stately pace from the Tower of London; sixty ladies of rank, dressed in the richest elegance of the day, followed on their palfreys, one after another, each leading by a silver chain a knight completely armed for tilting. Minstrels and trumpets accompanied them to Smithfield amidst the shouting population; there the queen and her fair train received them. The ladies dismounted, and withdrew to their allotted seats; while the knights mounted their steeds, laced their helmets, and prepared for the encounter. They tilted at each other till dark. They all then adjourned to a sumptuous banquet, and dancing consumed the night, till fatigue compelled every one to seek repose. The next day the warlike sport commenced; many were unhorsed; many lost their helmets; but they all persevered with eager courage and emulation, till night again summoned them to their supper, dancing and concluding rest. The festivities were again repeated on the third day.'

But it was also in Smithfield that public executions took place and the terrible Smithfield burnings.

At the Reformation, the Priory was disbanded but the

hospital was saved, by the persuasion of Sir Richard Gresham, and granted to the City of London. The monastic buildings, the Lady Chapel, the Close and the Cloth Fair were sold to the Rich family, who held them until the early nineteenth century, but in Mary Tudor's brief reign, during which at least two hundred Protestants were burned at Smithfield, the Priory was granted as a home for Dominicans for a few years. Then, with the Protestant accession to the throne, the nave and many other parts of the building were pulled down, leaving, as a newly-established parish church, only the Choir, with some of the chapels, including the Lady Chapel, as well as the transepts, part of the south wall of the nave and the lovely west gateway.

The trade fairs had outlived their usefulness and soon only the names of the little streets and courts surrounding the old Priory – Cloth Fair (3) and Cloth Court – survived as reminders of the old days of the Cloth Fair.

By the time of Charles I the horse market had become a general market for cattle and sheep and the market dues went to the City of London. A large number of animals were slaughtered in West Smithfield and the meat sold to the butchers of Newgate, just to the west of the hospital, while a new Fair was established here, a wildly gay and roystering affair, where you could see the Patagonian Samson, General Jacko, the baboon, the wild beast show, sword swallowers and rope dancers and a dozen or more plays which were staged in the showmen's booths. Like the original Fair, it lasted for three days at first, but with the Restoration it was extended to fourteen days. However, by the time of Queen Anne, it had become so rowdy and riotous, as well as a pickpocket's paradise, that it was curtailed again to three days.

In 1830 the City Companies bought the ancient rights of the Fair and in 1855, after much petitioning for its closure, the Fair came to an end. That same year the cattle market was moved to Islington, where it remained until 1939, never again to be opened, and the Newgate traders moved into Sir Horace Jones's new Smithfield meat market buildings.

During these years the remains of Rahere's church were miserably neglected. The Lady Chapel became a dwelling house and then a printer's office. In part of the triforium above the south aisle a Nonconformist school was established. In the choir there was a fringe factory, which by 1833 was also occupying the Lady Chapel. In the north transept was a blacksmith's forge and the bays of the cloisters were used for stables.

Then, albeit very late in the day, the preservationists set to work. Gradually the artisans and the stable keepers were bought out, the Lady Chapel was rebuilt, and within the last hundred years what remains of the church of St Bartholomew-The-Great has been restored. The entrance path to the west front, which runs alongside the tree-shaded graveyard, has been cut down to the level of the original nave and is where the south aisle ran.

The Norman arches of the church you see today are magnificent and Rahere's beautiful, canopied tomb is still there, on the north side of the sanctuary, close to the high altar, his effigy painted in the brilliant medieval colours of red, blue and gold, while night and day two red lanterns glow beside it, casting a solemn light on his face.

Through the years St Bartholomew's Hospital, his great and lasting achievement, has steadily held its place as one of the most distinguished in the country. The fame of its ever-open doors has spread through the whole world, a living memory to the gentle Rahere, who laboured so long and patiently for the sick and poor.

VISIONS AT THE CHARTERHOUSE

The meat market adjoins Smithfield to the north, and through it runs Charterhouse Street. Walking a few yards along it east-wards, Charterhouse Square lies on the north side, with the ancient buildings of the Charterhouse (4), in the north-east corner.

This was the site of the old Pardon churchyard, established during the fourteenth century by Ralph Stratford, the Bishop of London, for some of the thousands of victims of the terrible Black Death, which devastated the country in 1348. Here he built a small chapel, where masses were said for the dead, and as the plague still raged, Sir Walter de Manny bought more land from the brothers of St Bartholemew's, to extend the graveyard: and here, according to Stow, no less than 50,000 plague victims were buried.

The Bishop's successor bequeathed money for the establishment of a monastery of the strict and comfortless Carthusian order at the Pardon churchyard, to which Sir Walter de Manny added valuable endowments: and it was at this monastery that, many years later, Sir Thomas More, as a young man, stayed, 'religiously living there without vow about four years'.

Then came the Reformation and the dissolution of the monasteries. Many of the monks of the Charterhouse refused to acknowledge King Henry as head of the Church. The Prior, John Houghton, was sent to the Tower of London and with two other Carthusians were hanged, drawn and quartered at Tyburn. As they left the Tower for their last journey, Sir Thomas More, already a prisoner and awaiting his execution, stood at the window of his cell, with his cherished daughter, Margaret Roper. 'Dost thou not see, Meg,' he said, 'that these blessed fathers be now as cheerfully going to their deaths, as bridegrooms to their marriage.'

The remains of the Prior's body were impaled over the entrance gate of the Charterhouse, and this final indignity gave many more Carthusians the courage to resist the new order, although knowing full well what their fate would be.

But during these fateful weeks, many miracles took place at the monastery. There were visitations from monks already dead, urging their living brothers to remain true to their faith, and giving them the courage to face their martyrdom.

The lamps of the church were usually lit only on festival days, but one dark winter's night, as they were burying one of their members by a dim candle-light, a sudden flash of heavenly flame flared from the altar which, with a celestial brilliance, set all the lamps alight: and during the next few weeks sixteen more of their number were put to death.

Notwithstanding these heavenly portents, the monastery was dissolved by the Reformation decree and the few remaining monks fled to Bruges.

The building at this time comprised little more than a number of cells, a chapel, chapter-house and cloisters built round a quadrangle, and for a few years they were left to decay, the King himself taking some of the timber and glass, as well as trees from the orchard and carp from the fish-pond, for his new palace at Chelsea. Then he granted the remains to Lord North, who built the magnificent Great Hall and turned the monastery into a private mansion. Here he entertained Queen Elizabeth for a few days, on her journey from Hatfield to London at the time of her accession, and again for three or four days in 1561, but his hospitality was so lavish that it is said to have crippled him financially for the rest of his life, which he was obliged to spend 'in privacy'.

His son made many palatial additions to the building and then sold it to the Duke of Norfolk, who was later executed, and ultimately it was bought by Sir Thomas Sutton, the immensely wealthy philanthropist, who was said to have been the original of Ben Jonson's *Volpone*. In 1611 Sir Thomas converted the Charterhouse into a hospital for eighty aged men and for the education of the sons of poor parents.

The school, which grew to become a distinguished public school, moved to Godalming in 1867, but some forty elderly men, bachelors and widowers, still live in the Charterhouse, amidst the ancient courts and cloisters, Lord North's splendid hall being now their dining room.

Although the Charterhouse suffered grievously during the bombing of World War Two, the damage has now been repaired.

THE KNIGHTS OF ST JOHN

Turn back westwards along Charterhouse Street to St John Street, which is the first turning on the right. Walk up it a few yards and take the left branch, St John's Lane. You have moved into Clerkenwell and suddenly, spanning the street, you are confronted with the magnificent St John's Gate **(5)**, an astonishing survival to find in this sadly drab corner of London. The gate was once the south gate of the Priory of St

St John's Gate, Clerkenwell.
By kind permission of the St John's Gate Museum, Clerkenwell
Photographed by J Taylor

John of Jerusalem, the London home of the Knights Hospitallers. The order was founded in 1092 to offer hospitality to pilgrims visiting the Holy Land and to tend the sick and wounded Crusaders, but in the 12th century they joined with the Knights Templars and became a fighting order to defend Jerusalem.

The Clerkenwell Priory was established in 1148, and though it was severely damaged by Wat Tyler's rebels two hundred years later, it was gradually restored to its former grandeur.

The courtyard covered what is now *St John's Square, on the north side of the Clerkenwell Road,* which was cut through it, and their church of St John (6) still stands in the north-east corner of the square. The first church, like the Temple church, was circular, after the pattern of the Church of the Holy Sepulchre in Jerusalem, but this too was burnt down during the Peasants' Revolt, although the nearby Charterhouse was spared.

Early in the sixteenth century Prior Thomas Docwra rebuilt the church, this time in a rectangular form, and also the present gatehouse, and it was over this ground that in 1237 the Knights Hospitallers rode on their way to the Holy Land. 'They set out from their house in Clerkenwell', recorded Matthew Paris, 'and proceeding in good order, with about thirty shields uncovered, with spears raised, and preceded by their banner, through the midst of the city, towards the bridge, that they might obtain the blessing of the spectators, and, bowing their heads with their cowls lowered, commended themselves to the prayers of all.'

With the Reformation, the Order of St John of Jerusalem was suppressed. The last Prior, Sir William Weston, is said to have died of a broken heart, but many of the surviving knights retired to Malta. The Priory buildings were appropriated by the Crown but were unoccupied and gradually fell into decay and desolation, the stones being taken away, over the years, for the building of many of the great houses of Clerkenwell, during the days when it was a fashionable suburb: but the Gateway survived unspoiled.

A greater part of the church was blown up with gun-powder and much of the stone taken by Protector Somerset for the building of Somerset House. Then it came into the possession of Lady Burleigh, who re-opened it in 1623 as a private chapel: but when it passed to the Earl of Aylesbury, he used part of the magnificent crypt, partly Norman, partly Early English, which had survived all the vicissitudes of the years, as a wine cellar.

By the early eighteenth century it was a Presbyterian meeting-house but during the Sacheverell riots it was again gutted. A few years later, however, it was rescued and became a parish church: and as such it remained for the next two hundred years. As the resident population of Clerkenwell declined, the parish was amalgamated with that of the nearby St James of Clerkenwell Green (7), and in 1931 it was handed back to the Order, to become once more the Grand Priory Church of the Order of St John. It was gravely damaged by incendiary bombs in 1941 but the restoration and rebuilding were completed in 1958.

Although Docwra's gateway is all that remains of the ancient Priory, many legends of eighteenth-century literary London have grown up round it, for it was here that Edward Cave came to live, setting up his printing press and launching his famous *Gentleman's Magazine*, which Dr Johnson so admired, before he ever left Lichfield. Johnson was given an introduction to Cave, who was quick to recognize his genius, and here from 1737 Johnson worked for several years, until he had established himself. But at first he was so poor that he was considered too shabby to be seen, and had to work and eat his dinner behind a screen. Yet he persuaded Cave to allow an amateur performance of Fielding's *Mock Doctor*, in order that his young friend David Garrick, who had come to London with him, could show his talent. With Garrick in the lead, several of the printers took minor parts, and Cave was so impressed with his acting that from that day he was safely launched on the London stage.

After Cave's death, when the new owners of the magazine transferred its offices, in 1781, to Lion Passage, Fleet Street, the Old Jerusalem tavern was established in the gateway and flourished until, in 1831, the revived Order of St John bought it.

SALLY IN OUR ALLEY

A few yards westwards down the Clerkenwell Road brings you to Clerkenwell Green. There is little enough left to remind us of its traditional gaiety and the days of its seventeenth-century grandeur, when the Green was surrounded by the mansions of the rich and noble, *yet St James' church* (**7**), *on its little hill on the north side of the Green*, still has the air of a country church and evokes a strong feeling that all the surrounding commercialism is but lightly laid upon a place which has seen if not happier, certainly more romantic days. Old Izaak Walton lived close by and two of his sons are buried in the church-yard. Early in the eighteenth century Henry Carey, music master and song writer for the old Sadlers Wells theatre and the author of *Sally in our Alley*, was also a resident. The story goes that Carey was inspired to write the song after watching a shoemaker's apprentice and his sweetheart on their day's holiday. He followed them, as the lad treated his girl to all the amusements he could afford, which included a visit to the poor madmen in Bedlam, which was close by, and all the other sights round about – the puppet shows and bookshops, old clothes stalls and second-hand furniture shops. Then he took her to the Farthing Pye House and feasted her on buns, cheese-cakes, stuffed beef and bottled ale.

Carey was charmed with the contented simplicity of their courtship and wistfully envious of their happiness. He was a lonely man, the illegitimate son of the Marquis of Halifax, and in 1743, in a sudden mood of depression, and with only one halfpenny left in his pocket, he hanged himself.

The Clerks' Well, around which, during the Early Middle Ages, the parish clerks of London used to gather each year to perform their mystery plays, and from which the Brothers of St John's Priory obtained their supply of water, was about a hundred yards from the west end of St James' church.

Return to Cock Lane by going south down Farringdon Road, and turning left down Snow Hill.

SCRATCHING FANNY OF COCK LANE

It was from Clerkenwell that one of the strangest of all London ghost stories began to circulate. It centred on Cock Lane (**8**), which runs from Giltspur Street westwards, just behind St Sepulchre's church. The year was 1760. Mr Parsons, the

Parish clerk, was attending morning service at St Sepulchre's. He noticed a young woman and an older man, whom he had not seen before, standing in the aisle, and showed them into a pew. Afterwards the man thanked Mr Parsons and asked him if he knew of a lodging, whereupon Parsons offered him a room in his own house, close by in Cock Lane.*

The man, a widower, was named Kent and his companion was his sister-in-law, Miss Fanny. After the death of his wife – Fanny's sister – Kent had sent for Fanny to come to London from her comfortable home in Norfolk, to join him. Kent had already inherited his wife's money, and since the law would not allow him to marry her sister, Fanny became his mistress, having first, at Kent's suggestion, made a will leaving him her own money.

They moved into Cock Lane and Mr Parsons, always hard up, borrowed a considerable sum of money from his new tenant, which he seemed loth to repay.

Kent had to leave Fanny for a short time, to attend a wedding in the country, and while he was away Fanny took Parsons' small daughter, Elizabeth, a child of about eleven years of age, to sleep with her in her bed. During the night they heard scratchings and faint tappings, for which there seemed no accounting. Neighbours were called in to listen and the mystery deepened. Some said the sounds were made by a neighbouring cobbler, but they continued on Sundays when he was not working. Others declared it was a ghost behind the wainscoting, and the parish clergyman was asked to exorcize it, but he was not convinced of the existence of a ghost and declined.

Fanny was terrified, convinced that the sounds came from the spirit of her dead sister, warning her of her own imminent death. Night after night the mysterious sounds recurred and when Kent returned to London the couple moved to Bartlett Court in Clerkenwell. Very soon after this, Fanny was taken ill with smallpox. Kent sent for her elder sister, who although living in Pall Mall, had no idea of Fanny's whereabouts since she had left home. She came at once, relieved to find her sister

*It became Number 20 Cock Lane and survived until 1979, when it was pulled down and the site cleared for office building.

again and glad that she appeared to be recovering. But two days later Fanny died. Her sister attended the funeral at St John's church, yet as the coffin was taken down to the crypt, she was puzzled to see that it bore no name, and she wondered why she had not been allowed to see Fanny before the lid was screwed down.

For some eighteen months all was quiet in Cock Lane, but then the noises began again, coming from beneath the bed of little Elizabeth. Parsons still had not paid his debt to Kent, who, despite his considerable inheritance from Fanny, was pressing for it. Parsons developed a morbid hatred for him. He alleged that his daughter had become possessed of Fanny's ghost, who was responsible for the new outbreak of tappings. Then he said that, with the help of a nurse, Mary Frazer, he had established a communication with Fanny, by telling her to rap once if the answer were 'Yes' and twice if it were 'No': and by this means he had gained the information that she had died from arsenical poisoning administered by Kent, while she was lying ill with smallpox.

News of the ghostly noises spread through the city and soon hundreds of people were coming to Cock Lane to hear the unhappy ghost struggling to tell its story to little Elizabeth. Although there were a few doubters, most people believed firmly in the existence of the ghost, particularly when the child declared that she had actually seen it. She was moved into a neighbour's house, but the rappings from her bed continued, and eventually Horace Walpole arrived there, with the Duke of York, Lady Northumberland, Lady Mary Coke and Lord Hertford. They set out from the Opera, changed their clothes at Northumberland House, and arrived all in one hackney coach. Walpole, in letters to Horace Mann and George Montague, describing the visit, said that it was raining that evening in torrents, yet Cock Lane and the house itself, a wretchedly small and miserable place, which was borrowed and to which the ghost had adjourned, was so crowded that they could hardly make their way in, until people recognized the Duke of York and fell back for him to pass through.

They found fifty people in the room and they stayed until half-past one in the morning, but they heard nothing, and went away convinced that it was all a fraud, despite the promise that the ghost would appear at seven o'clock that morning.

Yet there were still many believers. Mrs Montagu, writing to Mrs Robinson, said '. . .you could never conceive that the most bungling performance of the silliest imposture could take up the attention and conversation of all the fine world'.

Still the curious and gullible flocked to Cock Lane, and while they waited provisions for them all were sent in from the neighbouring taverns and ale houses, which were doing splendid business, both for themselves and Parsons.

Yet since the ghost was said to be informing the world of a serious crime, the parish clergyman decided to invite a group of gentlemen, 'eminent in rank and character', which included Dr Johnson, to make a special investigation at his own house. On the night of February 1st, 1762, the girl was put to bed by several ladies and about 10 o'clock that evening the gentlemen entered the room. They waited for an hour, but nothing happened and they went downstairs again. They questioned Parsons closely but he denied any knowledge of the fraud. Then came a message from the ladies that they had heard the noises and Elizabeth said she felt the spirit on her, like a mouse on her back. Dr Johnson asked her to hold her hands out of the bed, whereupon the knockings ceased, and he expressed his first doubts, but Parsons said that if they went to the vault of St John's, where Fanny's coffin lay, the spirit would speak to them, by raps on the lid. Along they went, and at one o'clock in the morning descended to the vault. No sound came. The spirit had let both them and Parsons down. They returned to Elizabeth but could get no confession from her, and about two or three o'clock in the morning, when she asked to be allowed to go home with her father, they let her go.

Dr Johnson declared that the whole business was a fraud and published his account in the *Gentleman's Magazine*: but the believers were appalled at such blasphemy. Elizabeth was moved from one house to another in the neighbourhood and still the knockings came. Then her bed was suspended like a hammock, four or five feet from the ground, and her hands and feet were bound. There were no noises.

The next day she was pressed again to confess and was told that if the knockings and scratches were not heard any more, she and her father and mother would be sent to Newgate. The strange sounds were heard again, but some, perhaps with hindsight, said they were different from the earlier ones. A servant kept secret watch in Elizabeth's room and saw her hide a small wooden board under her stays. The trick was revealed and Kent took action. Parsons and his wife, with the nurse Frazer, were brought before Lord Mansfield at the Guildhall. For the defence it was suggested that the terrified Elizabeth used the board only on the last occasion, after the threat of Newgate, being desperate that some sort of noise should be produced.

The plea was unsuccessful and Parsons was sentenced to stand three times in the pillory at the end of Cock Lane and serve two years in the King's Bench prison, his wife was given a year's imprisonment and Mary Frazer was committed to the Bridewell for six months, with hard labour. Yet Parsons never confessed and many remained sympathetic to him, even raising a public subscription for him, while Elizabeth survived two husbands and lived on until 1806.

There is a tail piece to this strange story. Some years later, while Wykeham Archer was drawing in the crypt of St John's, the sexton's boy pointed to one of the coffins and told him it belonged to Scratching Fanny, the Cock Lane ghost. Archer removed the lid and found in it the body of a young woman. 'The face,' he said, 'was perfect, handsome, oval, with an aquiline nose', but over the body was a greyish-white fatty substance. It had become adipocere. 'Will not arsenic produce adipocere?' wrote Archer. 'She is said to have been poisoned, although the charge is understood to have been disproved.'

FROM NEWGATE TO TYBURN

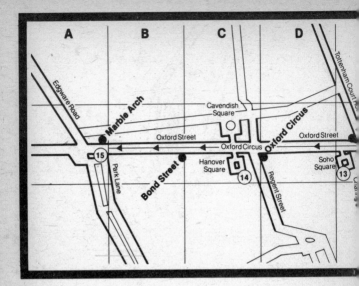

See Ely Place and St Etheldreda's on map for section B.

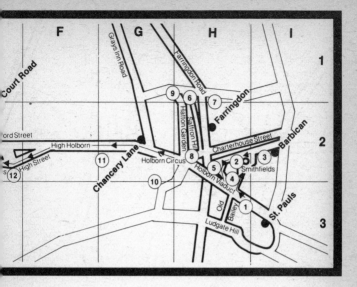

C

C

BUSES
Ludgate Hill: 4, 6, 9, 11, 15, 18, 23, 141, 502, 513.
Farringdon Street: 23, 46, 141, 168.
Holborn Viaduct: 8, 22, 25, 501.
High Holborn: 8, 19, 22, 25, 501, 38.
New Oxford Street – Oxford Street: 1, 7, 8, 25, 73.
Oxford Street – Marble Arch: 1, 6, 7, 8, 12, 13, 15, 73, 88, 133, 137, 159, 500, 616.

This is only a rough guide to the buses and you may need to consult the London Transport Bus Maps.

UNDERGROUNDS
St Paul's
Farringdon
Chancery Lane
Holborn
Tottenham Court Road
Oxford Circus
Bond Street
Marble Arch

FROM NEWGATE TO TYBURN

If you walk from Newgate Street westwards over Holborn Viaduct, along Holborn, High Holborn, New Oxford Street and Oxford Street to Marble Arch, you will be crossing the same ground that for five hundred years, from the thirteenth century until 1783, the death cart took, carrying condemned criminals from Newgate prison (1) to their hanging at Tyburn: but the Holborn Viaduct was not built until 1869, by which time the Tyburn hangings had ceased. The old route from the prison to Holborn was along Giltspur Street (2) and through Smithfield (3) to Cow Lane. Then the procession crossed the old Holborn Bridge over the Fleet ditch and began the steep ascent of Holborn Hill, which was sometimes called Heavy Hill. To 'ride up Heavy Hill' meant that a man's misbehaviour might one day lead him to Tyburn, while 'going west' meant that he was literally on the way there.

There were several other gallows in London and at first Tyburn was reserved for the upper classes, though not for long. The first hangings at Tyburn were a little to the west of the later site of the gallows, where the western tributary of the Tyburn river crossed what is now the Bayswater Road. The brook was lined with elm trees and the first recorded hanging was on one of these trees, when Roger de Mortimer, a lover of Edward II's wife, Queen Isabella, was dragged there on a hurdle, hanged, drawn and quartered and left there for several days. Later the place of execution was moved to the end of the Edgware Road, where today the Marble Arch stands (15).

Until the sixteenth century, Holborn had changed very little since early medieval times. The death cart passed through the Holborn Bars, which had been set up in the thirteenth century, to mark the City boundary, and entered a roughly made highway from which there was a vista of green fields, gardens and orchards, all the way to the village of St Giles, where there was an uninterrupted view of the hills of Hampstead and Highgate.

Entering Holborn, the condemned men passed on their right Ely House, the palace of the Bishops of Ely, with its beautiful gardens famous for their roses and strawberries, their orchards,

The Church of St Etheldreda, Ely Place.
British Tourist Authority

vineyards and cattle pastures, which stretched almost as far as Clerkenwell. Adjoining it was the chapel of St Etheldreda (8), the patron saint of Ely. St Etheldreda, who died in 679, was queen of East Anglia and founded the Abbey of Ely. She was twice married, and twice, it is said, maintained her virginity. According to Bede, she died of a tumour in the throat, caused by an early love of necklaces, which is the reason for the

60

chapel's association with St Blaise, the skilful physician who
entered the Church and in the fourth century became Bishop
of Armenia and was martyred for his faith. While he was in
prison he saved the life of a boy who was choking to death after
swallowing a fish bone, and ever after, on St Blaise's day,
February 3rd, people suffering from a disease of the throat
came to St Etheldreda's, where two consecrated candles, held
in the form of a cross, were laid on their throats to effect a cure.

In the second half of the sixteenth century, Christopher
Hatton, with whom Queen Elizabeth was so infatuated, had a
fancy to live in Ely House, which the Bishops seldom used at
this time. He established himself in the gate house and his
family were eventually to come into possession of the house
and gardens. By the end of the seventeenth century they had
sold them for the development of Hatton Garden (**9**), St Cross
Street and Kirby Street, but the beautiful old church of St
Etheldreda has survived and on the site of the old house is the
eighteenth-century Ely Place.

Near Fetter Lane (**10**) was John Gerard's garden, full of
plants, herbs and fruit trees, most of which he had collected
from the nearby fields. He published his herbal in 1597 and it
was the following year that Stow wrote that High Holborn,
leading from the Bars to St Giles, was very full of pits and

Hatton Garden.

sloughs. The prisoners passed the gardens of Gray's Inn on their right, of Staple Inn and Lincoln's Inn on their left.

The parish of St Giles-in-the-Fields (12) had grown up round the leper hospital built here in the twelfth century and dedicated to St Giles, the patron saint of lepers, and here, at the hospital gates, condemned prisoners were offered a last bowl of ale, while the great bell of St Giles' church tolled a passing knell.

In 1605, John Dowes, a merchant tailor, left £50 to the church of St Sepulchre (4), for the services of the clerk to visit the condemned prisoners on the night before the execution and again, early the following morning. He was there 'to ring certain tolls with a handbell and was afterwards, in a most Christian manner, to put them in mind of their present condition and approaching end, and to exhort them to be prepared, as they ought to be, to die.'

It therefore became a tradition for the clerk to walk along to the prison, ring his bell outside the door of the condemned cell and read aloud this homily.

> 'All you that in the condemned hold do lie
> Prepare you, for tomorrow you shall die;
> Watch all, and pray, the hour is drawing near
> That you before the Almighty must appear;
> Examine well yourselves, in time repent,
> That you may not to eternal flames be sent.
> And when St Sepulchre's bell to-morrow tolls,
> The Lord above have mercy on your souls.
>
> Past twelve o'clock.'

There is thought to have been a secret tunnel under the roadway, between the crypt of St Sepulchre's and the prison, along which prisoners were taken who wished to receive the last sacrament.

The following morning, when the wretched men were in the death cart, they were drawn first to the church, in accordance with the terms of Dowe's bequest, where the clerk was waiting for them, again tolling his bell and begging all the onlookers to join with him in prayers for the criminals.

'All good people, pray heartily unto God for these poor

sinners, who are now going to their death, for whom the great bell doth toll.'

And to the condemned men he cried: 'You that are condemned to die, repent with lamentable tears; ask mercy of the Lord, for the salvation of your own souls, through the merits, death and passion of Jesus Christ, who now sits at the right hand of God, to make intercession for as many of you as penitently return unto him.'

For many years after this, each criminal was then presented with a nosegay. One of the last to receive his flowers was Sixteen-String Jack, the highwayman who had once been coachman to Lord Sandwich, at his house in the south-east corner of Bedford Row, and was hanged in 1774. By this time the old church had been almost destroyed during the Great Fire and rebuilt, but the ceremony continued.

J T Smith in his *Nollekens and His Times* says: 'I remember well, when I was in my eighth year, Mr Nollekens calling at my father's house in Great Portland Street, and taking me to Oxford Street, to see the notorious Jack Rann, commonly called Sixteen-String Jack, go to Tyburn to be hanged . . . The criminal was dressed in a pea-green coat with an immense nosegay in his button-hole, which had been presented to him at St Sepulchre's steps; and his nankeen small-clothes, we were told, were tied at each knee with sixteen strings.'

Jack had boasted that his sixteen strings represented the sixteen times he had been tried and acquitted, for he was a crafty worker, but his luck ended when he robbed Princess Amelia's chaplain, the Reverend Dr Bell, in Gunnersbury Lane.

THE BLUE BOAR, HOLBORN

By the seventeenth century there was another stopping place on the way to the gallows, although only for the more gentlemanly prisoners. This was the Blue Boar (**11**), on the south side of High Holborn, where they were offered a glass of sherry.

This coaching inn was eventually merged with the adjacent George and became known as the George and Blue Boar, but it disappeared at the end of the coaching days and the Inns of Court Hotel, which has also now gone, was built in its place. Today, Number 285 High Holborn stands on the site.

There is a story of a strange meeting at the Blue Boar during the time that King Charles I was being held at Hampton Court by Cromwell. One of the King's attendants was a Cromwellian spy, in touch with another spy who was acting as servant at a house in Seething Lane, which was the secret meeting place of the Scottish Commissioners who were hoping to come to terms with the King, invade England and oust the Independents.

From Hampton Court the attendant reported to Cromwell's secret service that he had reason to believe that a royalist plot was being hatched with the Scots: and they would probably find out more about it from a letter he had seen the King writing to the Queen, who by then was in Paris. That letter, he said, would be sewn up in the messenger's saddle. The man would be arriving in London, at the Blue Boar in Holborn, that night, by coach, carrying the saddle with him: and he would be riding down to Dover as soon as he had hired his horse from the inn. The messenger, said the spy, knew nothing about the hidden letter, but its whereabouts were known to a royalist agent at Dover.

When Cromwell received the spy's message, he decided to investigate for himself. That dark December night, two days before Christmas, he and Ireton, disguising themselves as troopers, and taking with them only one man, duly arrived at the Blue Boar. They passed their time in one of the drinking stalls, with their cans of beer, while their man waited and watched in the courtyard. About ten o'clock he reported that a man carrying a saddle had just arrived on the incoming coach. They waited until he had hired his horse and saddled it: and as he was leading it away, Cromwell and Ireton approached with drawn swords. Quietly they told him that they had orders to search everyone entering or leaving the inn, but as he looked like an honest man, they would search only his saddle. Unprotesting, the messenger handed it over. Cromwell and Ireton took it to the room where they had been drinking, while the messenger stood chatting to their man in the courtyard. Quickly they found the letter and returned the saddle to the messenger, assuring him that all was well. He rode away, still having no idea that anything was amiss, while Cromwell and Ireton read the King's letter, in which he confided to the Queen that he was planning to ally himself with the Scots and English Presbyterians against Cromwell's party. It sealed his fate. Until this time, his confinement had been relatively tolerable, but once Cromwell realized that they were now never likely to come to reasonable terms, he determined on harsher measures.

The next morning, the King found himself under close guard and was allowed no more visitors. At the same time all cavaliers in London were ordered to leave the city within twenty-four hours and King Charles, whose fate might have been very different if the letter had never been discovered at the Blue Boar, was doomed.

JONATHAN WILD'S HOUSE

By the eighteenth century, the journey from Newgate to St Giles, in the dismal death cart, was very different in aspect from the earlier years, for the most appalling slums had developed at either end of Holborn, around Newgate and St Giles.

Field Lane, running from the foot of Holborn Hill north-wards, was one of the worst spots in London, the haunt of thieves and criminals of all kinds. As late as 1837, Dickens described it in *Oliver Twist*. 'Near to the spot on which Snow Hill (5) and Holborn meet, there opens, upon the right hand as you come out of the City, a narrow and dismal alley, leading to Saffron Hill. In the filthy shops are exposed for sale huge bunches of pocket-handkerchiefs of all sizes and patterns, for here reside the traders who purchase them from pickpockets. Hundreds of these handkerchiefs hang dangling from pegs outside the windows or flaunting from the doorposts, and the shelves within are piled with them . . . Here the clothes-man, the shoe-vamper and the rag-merchant display their goods as sign-boards to the petty thief, and stores of old iron and bones, and heaps of mildewy fragments of woollen-stuff and linen, rust and rot in the grimy cellars.'

Northwards from Field Lane, running from Charterhouse Street to the Clerkenwell Road and parallel with the Fleet ditch, was Saffron Hill (6), once part of the Ely House garden, where the saffron grew, which had quickly deteriorated into an overcrowded slum as evil as Field Lane. Close by, only a few houses to the east of Saffron Hill, was the notorious West Street, and Number 3, on the north-west side of the Fleet ditch (once the Red Lion tavern) had become a lodging house for thieves and prostitutes.

It was an extraordinary old place, said to have been built in the sixteenth century and sometimes known as Jonathan Wild's house, although when that notorious rogue was finally arrested and sent to Tyburn, he was living in fine style, in a house in Old Bailey, under the very eyes of the law. His means of livelihood was to organize a gang of thieves, who sold their spoils to him. Then, advertising himself as the 'thief-taker', he guaranteed to the victims to find their stolen goods for them, and received a handsome reward when he delivered them.

Jack Sheppard often hid in the house, although it was frequently searched by the police. The place was full of artfully contrived trap-doors and sliding panels, secret cupboards and bricked-in recesses, all of which provided excellent hiding places for men on the run, and a secret door in one of the attics led over the roof of the next door house to the comparative safety of the rapidly worsening slum of Saffron Hill, while the Fleet ditch, which ran along the back of the house, was a convenient place to dispose of dead bodies and other incriminating evidence.

When the place was pulled down, in 1844, a skull and piles of human bones were found in the cellar, grim evidence of the crimes that the horrible old house had seen.

THE ROOKERIES OF ST GILES

After the George and Blue Boar in Holborn, there was no New Oxford Street as yet, but the death cart made its way through the appalling slums and rookeries of St Giles, which developed with devastating speed during the early years of the eighteenth century and stretched from St Giles' church as far as Great Russell Street. Here was a congestion of flimsy, ramshackle buildings, hurriedly thrown up by speculative builders, to house the flood of Irish labourers and English country folk who flocked to London at this time, and for whom there was no other accommodation. In the most squalidly insanitary conditions, they crowded, sometimes seven or eight to a room, living in abject poverty and sustained by cheap gin.

The drink had been introduced from Holland by William of Orange and by this time was distilled from English corn. For some time its manufacture was encouraged because, according to Defoe, it consumed such large quantities of corn that the farmers and large landowners reaped handsome profits. It was cheaper than beer and during the 1730s and 40s there were said to be between six thousand and seven thousand gin shops in London alone. The poor drank so much of it that they died in their thousands, and Hogarth's grim picture *Gin Lane*, drawn in St Giles, shows how terrible the conditions were.

So the death cart moved on into the mile-long Oxford Street, which at one time was known as Tyburn Lane. At the corner with Tottenham Court Road there was a parish boundary stone and here the charity boys of St Giles' parish who had earned a flogging were whipped, so that, when they grew up, they might remember the place, and 'be competent to give evidence should any dispute arise with the neighbouring parishes'.

THE LAST MILE TO TYBURN

Soho Square (13) had been built soon after the Restoration and by 1717 the building of Hanover Square (14) and Cavendish Square were under way, but Oxford Street was still a lonely, muddy country lane, with only a few isolated, unimportant dwellings along the north side. It had an evil reputation for footpads and cut-throats, so that few people ventured along it after dark.

The squares remained high fashion throughout the century but the development of Oxford Street was held up because it was still the route to the Tyburn hangings. As early as 1720

John Strype mentioned that plans had been discussed for moving the gallows to some other spot – such as Kingsland – in order to save the residents of the squares from the annoyance of the noisy crowds that collected in Oxford Street to watch the procession to the Tyburn gallows. But nothing was done until 1783, when they were at last removed and the hangings took place outside Newgate prison, and later within its walls.

In the meantime, the residents of the squares turned their backs on Oxford Street, and the short access roads were barred by posts and rails.

The hangings took place about every six weeks and there were sometimes as many as fifteen condemned men in the cart. Crowds always lined the route of the procession and hanging day became something of a public holiday.

The condemned men reacted variously, some putting on a show of bravado, others frankly terrified.

Swift in *Tom Clinch going to be hanged* described, in 1727, Tom's last journey from Newgate to Tyburn.

'As clever Tom Clinch, while the rabble was bawling,
Rode stately through Holborn to die in his calling,
He stopped at the "George" for a bottle of sack,
And promised to pay for it – when he came back.
His waistcoat, and stockings, and breeches were white,
His cap had a new cherry-ribbon to tie't;
And the maids to the doors and the balconies ran,
And cried "Lack-a-day! He's a proper young man!" '

The executioner claimed the right to the clothes of the condemned and the body was usually claimed by the surgeons, for dissection at the Surgeons' Hall.

There is a story of five men who were sentenced to hanging after the mysterious death, in 1447, of 'good Duke Humphrey'. They were duly hanged, cut down, divested of their clothes and their bodies prepared for dismemberment, when a reprieve arrived. The men miraculously revived, but the hangman, feeling he had been cheated, refused to give them back their clothes, so the five gentlemen walked back to the City stark naked.

One of the most bizarre executions at Tyburn was that of

Anne Turner, who, during the reign of James I, was indicted for complicity in the murder of Thomas Overbury. She was an attractive young widow who had become the mistress of Sir Arthur Maynwaring. They had little money but good connections and an introduction to the Court. Anne was a clever dressmaker and helped the ladies of the Court with their clothes. She knew all that was going on, received confidences discreetly and brewed nostrums to solve difficult love affairs: and amongst her secret brews was a yellow starch for the fashionable neck ruffs. Lord Chief Justice Coke therefore sentenced her to be 'hang'd at Tyburn in her yellow Ruff and Cuff, she being the first inventor of and wearer of that horrid garb'.

She obeyed and went to her death, watched by huge crowds, wearing a yellow starched lawn ruff. Her hands 'were bound with a black silk ribbon, as she desired; and a black veil, which she wore upon her head, being pulled over her face by the executioner, the cart was driven away, and she left hanging, in whom there was no motion at all perceived.'

The executioner also wore yellow starched cuffs for the occasion, 'which made many after that day, of either sex, to forbear the use of that coloured starch, till it at last grew generally to be detested and disused.'

Jack Ketch was the hangman from 1663 to 1686 and his name was used for most of his successors. In 1717 the Jack Ketch of the day, whose real name was William Marvell, was himself arrested for debt while awaiting the arrival of the death cart. The bailiff said he would wait while he finished his work, but the crowd, sympathetic to the prisoners, would have none of it and he was taken away. One of the spectators, a bricklayer, then offered to do the job, but they fell on him so furiously that in the end the prisoners were taken back to Newgate and their sentences commuted to penal servitude.

So bitterly hated was the hangman that it was about this time that some of the prisoners, presumably to cheat him of their clothes, took to going to Tyburn in their shrouds.

MEN WHO SURVIVED HANGING

During the reign of Queen Anne, John Smith, an alleged

burglar, was duly hanged, but after he had been swinging for a quarter of an hour, a reprieve arrived. He was cut down and his apparently lifeless body was bled – which would seem to have been the least efficacious of remedies – but notwithstanding, the story goes that he recovered.

In 1740 an even stranger case was recorded. Among five people executed that November, was a boy of seventeen, William Duell. He had been indicted for rape, robbery and murder, and convicted of rape. He was hung up by the neck for more than twenty minutes and then cut down. His body was then taken by hackney coach to the Surgeons' Company in Old Bailey. As they laid him on the dissecting table they heard a groan. The surgeons bled him and within a few minutes he was able to sit up, though he could not yet speak. A message was sent to the Sheriff and there was talk of sending him back to Tyburn, but by the late afternoon, the mob had got wind of what was intended and protested loudly. The surgeons kept him until midnight, by which time the crowds had dispersed, and then he was secretly taken back to Newgate. They wrapped him in blankets and gave him hot gruel. Soon he was able to speak and asked for more food, although he seemed to have no clear idea where he was. But two days later he had completely recovered.

The prison governor was at a loss to know what to do with him. He remained in Newgate for a time and people flocked to see him and ask how he had felt. He said he could remember nothing of his execution or even of his trial, but stories were spread that he had made wonderful discoveries about the nature of the world after death and seen many strange ghosts and apparitions.

How he survived is a mystery. It was suggested that he was not hung long enough, or the rope was wrongly placed or his body was too light, but the surgeons explained that all the time he was in Newgate he was in a high fever and delirious. He therefore suffered no fear and his feverish blood circulated so quickly that it took longer than usual to be stopped by suffocation.

The problem of what next to do with him was solved by deporting him for life.

More than forty years later, in 1782, the year before the last of the Tyburn hangings, there was another case of a man recovering on the surgeon's dissecting table. This was John Haynes, a housebreaker, in whom the surgeon, Sir William Blizzard, noticed signs of life only moments before it would have been too late to revive him. Sir William asked him about his sensation when the rope tightened about his neck at the moment of suspension, but the reply was not illuminating. 'The last thing I recollect was going up Holborn Hill in a cart,' he said. 'I thought then that I was in a beautiful green field, and that is all I remember till I found myself in your honour's dissecting-room.'

THE EXECUTION OF LORD FERRERS

In 1760 Lord Ferrers murdered his steward for giving evidence against him, when Lady Ferrers divorced him. He was committed to the Tower, tried by his peers and condemned by the House of Lords. He refused to travel in the death cart and was allowed to journey to Tyburn in his own carriage. On the morning of the execution he dressed himself in the silver-embroidered coat he had worn for his wedding, and at nine o'clock the procession left the Tower, with thousands of people lining the route.

First came a string of constables; then one of the sheriffs, in his chariot and six, the horses dressed with ribbons; next Lord Ferrers, in his landau and six, his coachman in tears. The second sheriff sat beside him and guards marched on either side. The second sheriff's empty carriage followed, and then a mourning coach and six, a hearse, the Chaplain of the Tower in his landau, and a company of Horse Guards.

The procession was held up by the crowds so frequently that it took two hours to reach the gallows, but when Lord Ferrers asked for a drink of wine, it was refused him.

As they drew near to Tyburn he presented the sheriff with his watch, gave five guineas to the Chaplain and took out another five guineas for the executioner. Slowly the coach made its way through the crowds at Tyburn. Again it was delayed for a few minutes but at last the coach door opened and Ferrers stepped out and mounted the scaffold, which at the expense of his family had been draped in mourning black cloth.

A newly contrived stage had been placed under the gallows, which was to be struck from beneath him. He knelt for the Chaplain's prayer and murmured, 'Lord, have mercy upon me, and forgive me my errors', his hands were bound and his face covered. The rope was placed round his neck and the signal given for the stage to be struck. It did not work. Ferrers' toes touched it, but the executioner and his assistant pulled his legs, and within four minutes he was dead.

He had made one last request – that his body should not be stripped, and the sheriff who had accompanied him promised that though his clothes must be taken off, his shirt should not.

'The decency ended with him,' said Horace Walpole. 'The sheriffs fell to eating and drinking on the scaffold, and helped up one of their friends to drink with them, as the body was still hanging, which it did above an hour', after which it was taken to the Surgeons' Hall for dissection.

The executioners fought for the rope, which was a marketable souvenir, the going rate being sixpence an inch, while the mob tore off the black draperies on the scaffold as relics.

DOCTOR DODD

Dr Dodd's execution was in 1777. 'The doctor, to all appearance, was rendered perfectly stupid from despair,' wrote Anthony Storer to George Selwyn. 'His hat flapped all round and pulled over his eyes, which were never directed to any object around, nor ever raised, except now and then lifted up in the course of his prayers. He came in a coach, and a very heavy shower of rain fell just upon his entering the cart, and another just at his putting on his nightcap. During the shower an umbrella was held over his head, which Gilly Williams, who was present, observed was quite unnecessary, as the doctor was going to a place where he might be dried . . .The executioner took both the doctor's hat and his wig off at the same time. Why he put on his wig again I do not know, but he did; and the doctor took off his wig a second time, and tied on his nightcap, which did not fit him; but whether he stretched that or took another, I could not perceive. He then put on his nightcap himself, and upon his taking it, he certainly had a smile on his countenance; and very soon afterwards there was an end of all his hopes and fears on this side of the grave . . . The body was hurried to the house of Davies, an under-taker in Goodge Street, Tottenham Court Road, where it was placed in a hot bath, and every exertion made to restore life, but in vain.'

Yet there had been plans, in which Dr Johnson had played a part, to help his escape from Newgate before execution day, for many of his friends felt that his sentence was too harsh. In a moment of despair at his mounting debts, he had forged the name of Lord Chesterfield, to whom he had been tutor, to a bond of £4,200, and although Chesterfield was willing to forgive him and the Doctor had begun to pay back the money, he was condemned.

For long after his death there was a legend that the hangman had been bribed to place the rope in a certain position under his ears, so that he would not suffocate, and that he was successfully revived at the house in Goodge Street by a celebrated surgeon and made his escape to the Continent.

THE HIGHWAYMEN

During the seventeenth and eighteenth centuries there was a tremendous increase in the number of highwaymen. After the Civil War a certain number of Royalists who had lost everything were said to have taken to the roads, as their only means of survival, which probably accounts for the myth of the 'Gentlemen of the Roads', but although some of them came from respectable backgrounds and maintained a superficial air of breeding, most of them were brutal ruffians, prepared to sell their associates to the law if it would save their own skins.

One of the most perfidious was Jemmy Witney who, recorded Narcissus Luttrell, offered to bring in eight men of his gang if he might have his pardon. His offer was rejected. Several were caught and he again offered to turn King's evidence, but he was tried and condemned to death. On January 28th, 1692 he and eight of his confederates were taken to Tyburn, but Witney was suddenly given ten days' reprieve and brought back to Newgate with a rope round his neck. They got no more information from him and within the ten days he was executed at Smithfield.

A few months later no less than eighty more highwaymen were awaiting trial, including several women.

The problem grew so serious that in 1773 the Bow Street magistrate, Sir John Fielding, wrote to David Garrick 'concerning the impropriety of performing *The Beggar's Opera*, which never was represented on the stage without creating an additional number of real thieves'.

Shakespeare had said much the same thing. 'How oft the sight of means to do ill deeds makes ill deeds done.'

Many people have been echoing the same thought ever since, but nothing is ever done about it, despite overwhelming evidence that it is true.

THE END OF THE TYBURN HANGINGS

Once the gallows were removed from Tyburn, Oxford Street became respectable. The pickpockets and footpads disappeared as the building of shops and houses proceeded quickly, and soon even the ghosts, whom so many had seen haunting the site of the old gibbet, faded away and were forgotten. But in front of Newgate prison in Old Bailey (1) the public hangings went on until 1868, and sightseers flocked there in their thousands.

Places in the windows of the houses overlooking the gallows sold for anything up to two guineas, and on one occasion a first floor was let for twelve guineas. Often the onlookers arrived the evening before and spent the night playing cards, drinking and singing. Sometimes as many as eighty thousand people were packed into the narrow streets surrounding the prison and once, when a cart collapsed, on to which people had

The Holy Sepulchre Without Newgate.
Photographer: Nicholas Servian FIIP, Woodmansterne Ltd

crowded in order to get a better view, twenty-eight people were crushed to death.

The exact time for the execution was taken from the tolling of the bell at St Sepulchre's (**4**), the church that had seen so much of human degradation and suffering.

ST CECILIA AND ST SEPULCHRE'S CHURCH

St Sepulchre's (**4**) survived the bombing of World War Two and still has its beautiful Renatus Harris organ, which was built in 1677 and on which both Handel and Mendelssohn are said to have played, as well as Sir Henry Wood, when he was only twelve years old.

In 1955 the north chapel was dedicated as the memorial chapel of musicians, and on 22nd November each year, the day of St Cecilia, a special service and concert are held here, the concert continuing a three-hundred-year-old tradition of musical celebration of St Cecilia, which has been held in various parts of London.

Cecilia, said to have been the 'inventor of the organ', was a blind Roman Christian martyr, with whom an angel fell in love, because of her rare musical skills, and visited every night.

When she married, she told her husband that 'whether she was awake or asleep, the angel was ever beside her', and after he had been baptized in the Christian faith, he saw him with his own eyes, for the angel visitor brought them both a crown of martyrdom, which he had carried from Paradise.

FROM THE BANK OF ENGLAND TO THE TOWER OF LONDON

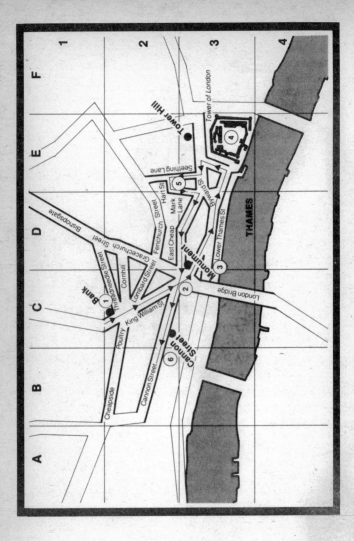

D

D

BUSES
Bank: 11, 21, 25, 43, 76, 133, 501, 502.
Cannon Street: 9, 513.
East Cheap/Tower Hill: 9.

This is only a rough guide to the buses and you may need to consult the London Transport Map.

UNDERGROUNDS
Bank
Monument
Cannon Street
Tower Hill

THE BANK OF ENGLAND

This walk begins in the very heart of the City of London. The area referred to as 'the Bank' is a triangular space with the Bank of England (1) along its north side, the Royal Exchange on the east and the Mansion House on the south-west, and it is reached by both the Northern and Central Underground lines, as well as many bus routes.

The idea for the formation of the Bank of England, the first joint stock bank in the country, was put forward by William Paterson in 1691, at a time when the Crown debt was £2,000,000, contracted during the long wars with France, and the government, already borrowing at exorbitantly high interest rates of some 20% or more, was in urgent need of another £1,200,000. Paterson said they would be able to offer loans at 8%. The capital to establish it was raised within ten days and it opened at first in the Grocers' Hall, moving to its present site in 1734.

The church of St Christopher le Stocks and more than twenty houses had to be demolished, but the burial ground was retained, to become the bank's central garden, and here,

The Bank of England (*left*) and the Royal Exchange (*centre*).
Marianne Taylor

soon after its establishment, permission was granted for one of the clerks, who was seven feet six inches tall, to be buried, in order to save his body from the grave robbers, who were prevalent during these years, snatching newly buried corpses to sell to the anatomists for dissection.

The original bank building was designed by George Sampson and the east and west wings were added a few years later by Sir Robert Taylor, but Sir John Soane was mainly responsible for the magnificent building of pillared courtyards and beautiful halls and court rooms which rose, seven storeys high and covering four acres, behind its massive walls.

In the years before World War Two, a good deal of the bank was rebuilt by Sir Herbert Baker, but Sir Robert Taylor's court room is still there and much of Soane's work remains.

The Royal Exchange is the third building on this site. The first Exchange was founded by the Elizabethan merchant and financier, Sir Thomas Gresham, and opened by Queen Elizabeth I in 1570. It was the first Renaissance building in the City, a long, four-storeyed building with a double balcony, built round a courtyard with covered walks supported by marble pillars, and the bell tower was surmounted by the Gresham family crest of a grasshopper. It was planned to rival the magnificence of the old Venetian Bourse, and with its hundred shops, it was soon the meeting place for merchants from all over Europe, as well as one of the sights of London for country visitors.

It was destroyed during the Great Fire of 1666, but within three years Edward Jerman had built a new and larger Exchange, in which the shops were soon let. This building was burned down in 1838, and the present Exchange, again in the classical style, with a Corinthian portico, central courtyard and covered walks, was built four or five years later, designed by Sir William Tite, but it is no longer full of shops, a large part being occupied by the head offices of the Guardian Royal Exchange Assurance Group.

The Mansion House, the official residence of the Lord Mayor of London, was built in 1753 by George Dance the Elder, but not without many difficulties, for the site was the old Stocks market, and when the builders began to dig the foundations they found underground springs and numbers of streams which ran into the course of the old Walbrook. The mansion had to be built on piles. Even so, it was so damp at first that the Common Council seriously considered abandoning it and finding a new site, but the trouble was cured when the central courtyard was covered.

THE CITY MONUMENT

From the Bank of England, cross over to King William Street and walk southwards to the City Monument (2), which was erected in 1671-7 to commemorate the Great Fire of London. This Doric column is 202 feet high, which is said to be the exact distance eastwards of the baker's shop in Pudding Lane, where the fire started.

Until recent years, the Monument has always been regarded as Wren's work, despite the fact that John Aubrey ascribed it to his friend Robert Hooke, the City Surveyor. It now seems that Aubrey was right, for Hooke's diary, not published until 1935, mentions it frequently and describes his talks with Wren about it.

Wren, we know, had originally designed a more elaborate monument, surmounted by a colossal statue of Charles II, a plan which was rejected, probably in favour of Hooke's, for in June, 1675, two years before the Monument was completed, Hooke recorded: 'At Sir Christopher Wren's but noe money nor favour. He seemed jealous of me.'

BILLINGSGATE

Continue down King William Street until you reach Lower Thames Street on your left. A few yards down is the Billingsgate fish market (3), the oldest of the City's produce markets, which has stood here for more than a thousand years. The market hall, designed by Sir Horace Jones and built in 1876, has been declared a protected building, but the market itself is shortly to move down river to the Isle of Dogs. The new market is now

The Monument.
Marianne Taylor

being built and it is hoped to be ready for occupation early in 1982.

Although archaeologists have found no real evidence, it is said that the first Celtic settlement of London was around here, built on the first rising ground above the estuary, where the little stream of the Walbrook joined the Thames. It consisted of a few mud huts surrounded by an earth wall, and was called Llyn-Din, the Hill by the Pool. About 400 BC, so the story goes, Belin, a Celtic king, rebuilt the wall and on the south side, along the river front, ordered a small landing place to be cut, with a wooden quay: and to enter the settlement from the quayside, a water gate was made in the wall, which was called Belinsgate.

Geoffrey of Monmouth declared that 'about four hundred years before Christ's nativity, Belin, a king of the Britons, built this gate and gave it its name and that when he was dead the royal body was burnt, and the ashes set over the gate in a vessel of brass, upon a high pinnacle of stone'.

In later years, less inventive historians than Geoffrey said that Billing was probably a city alderman who came into possession of the quay, but Stow's account of the fish landed at Billingsgate from the Thames, although historically accurate, sounds as legendary as anything that Geoffrey of Monmouth conceived. 'What should I speak of the fat and sweet salmon daily taken in this stream, and that in such plenty (after the time of the smelt is past) as no river in Europe is able to exceed it? But what store of barbels, trouts, chevens, perches, smelts, breams, roaches, daces, gudgeons, flounders, shrimps, eels etc are commonly to be had therein . . .'

THE TOWER OF LONDON

Ahead of you less than half a mile away is the Tower of London (**4**), dominated by its great central keep, the White Tower. Londoners were alarmed when King William began to build the White Tower. They had accepted him and he seemed prepared for reasonable cooperation and a recognition of their special rights and important powers, but the Tower was a sign that at the first sign of trouble, he was prepared to use force. They were even more concerned when, over the years, succeeding Norman and Plantagenet kings built a massive curtain wall, into which thirteen more towers were built and then an outer bailey with yet more towers in its wall, and finally surrounded it all with a wide moat.

'It was,' said William Fitzstephen, 'exceedingly great and strong, whose walls and bailey rise from very deep foundations; their mortar being mixed with the blood of beasts.'

Many people thought that the Tower was a relic of Roman times but this is a fallacy. William the Conqueror ordered Gundulf, his newly appointed Bishop of Rochester, who had already had a great deal of experience in stone building, to design the White Tower, and it is built partly of Kentish ragstone and partly of Norman limestone imported from Caen. But it is built against the south-east corner of the old Roman wall, parts of which are still visible, while some parts of the vast complex are built on Roman foundations.

During the thirteenth century, Henry III began to make this symbol of domination even stronger and more fearful by building additional fortifications along the river front, which included the Tower wharf and a water gateway from the Thames, over which he planned yet another defensive tower.

The citizens of London wondered what it portended, and it was in trepidation that they gathered on St George's day of 1240, for their prayers to the patron saint. That night the stones of the half-built wharf and the water gate collapsed and fell in the river. It had happened because of an exceptionally high spring tide, said the master of the builders, and work began again. But the following year, on the same day, precisely the same thing happened. All the masonry, bricks and rubble crashed into the river.

The people of London were exultant and wondered who their deliverer could be. And then one of the priests told them what had happened. That night of the second collapse, as he was passing the Tower, he had paused to watch the builders at work. As he stood there, he saw, to his amazement, the figure of a mitred archbishop, dressed in his episcopal robes and carrying his crozier, and he was attented by a clerk.

The priest saw the archbishop looking sternly and disapprovingly at the half-built gate and tower and heard him ask the workmen why they were being built. He did not hear the workmen's reply, but it clearly angered the archbishop, for he thereupon struck the stones with his crozier and they crumbled into a useless heap and fell into the river, just as they had the previous year.

The priest summoned up his courage to speak to the attendant clerk and ask him the name of the archbishop.

'He is Thomas à Becket – St Thomas the Martyr,' replied the clerk.

'And why has he done this?' asked the priest.

'St Thomas was a citizen of London and he dislikes these towers,' said the clerk, 'because they are being built against the wishes of the people of London and are a threat to their rights.'

Thereupon both St Thomas and the clerk vanished.

The story reached the ears of the King, and although he ordered the rebuilding to begin yet again, this time he played for safety and took the precaution of placing an oratory in his new tower, dedicated to St Thomas.

The Tower of London.
British Tourist Authority

In Tudor times the water-gate became known as Traitors' Gate and the Tower built over it – St Thomas's Tower – is named in memory of the later Saint Thomas – Sir Thomas More.

THE TOWER'S MYSTERIES AND GHOSTS

Scores of strange, unexplained stories about the Tower have arisen over the centuries. It was in the Council Chamber of the White Tower that Richard II formally renounced the throne, handing the sceptre and crown to his cousin, Henry of Lancaster. Richard remained a prisoner in the Tower, but less than a month later, on a dark October night, he was spirited away to Pontefract Castle, where, within a week or two, in mysterious circumstances, he died.

During the Wars of the Roses, Sir Henry Wyatt, father of the poet, was held in the Tower under appalling conditions, with no bed, no warm clothing and not enough food. One day a cat walked into his dungeon and Sir Henry took it in his arms to keep himself warm. From that time onwards, all through his imprisonment, the cat would call on him two or three times a day, sometimes bringing with her a welcome pigeon, which the gaoler, with no awkward questions asked, would cook for Sir Henry's dinner. Ever after he was devoted to cats, and when his portrait was painted, always insisted on having one included in the picture.

Poor, feeble-minded Henry VI was kept in the Wakefield Tower for years, after the rout of the Lancastrians, but he was a devout man and was said to have visions and the gift of prophecy. He, too, died mysteriously, on the night that Edward IV arrived triumphantly in London after the battle of Tewkesbury. Some said that he died of 'pure displeasure and melancholy' but many believed that he was stabbed to death by the King's brother, Richard, Duke of Gloucester, as he knelt at prayer in his oratory, for when his body was later laid before the altar of St Paul's cathedral, blood was seen to pour from it.

Later it was secretly moved to Chertsey Abbey, for burial 'without priest, clerk, torch or taper, singing or saying'. Again it bled. Some time after this, therefore, being venerated for his saintliness, Richard, perhaps in remorse, ordered King Henry's second burial, at Windsor.

Edward IV's mistress was Jane Shore, and after his death she lived under the protection of Edward's close friend, Lord Hastings. Edward IV's elder son, the twelve-year-old Prince Edward, was heir to the throne, and Richard, Duke of Gloucester, as Protector, arranged for him to be established in the royal apartments of the Tower, to await his coronation as Edward V. He then called a Council of State at the Tower, to discuss the final details of the coronation ceremony, and among those summoned was Hastings, who had already sworn fealty to the new boy King, thereby making himself a potential enemy of Richard, in his private plan to seize the throne for himself.

The night before the Council meeting, Hastings' loyal friend, Lord Stanley, had a terrible dream, foretelling Hastings' end, and warned him to stay away, but Hastings laughed away his fears and attended.

Richard arrived late at the meeting and acted calmly but strangely. Then he postponed the meeting for another hour, and when he returned he appeared in a frenzy of rage. Suddenly he accused Lord Hastings of having plotted by necromancy with Elizabeth Woodville, Edward IV's widow, and Jane Shore, the witch, to bring about his death. He bared his withered arm, which had been deformed since childhood, and declared that the disability had been caused by the sorcery and witchcraft of Jane. Thereupon he banged furiously upon the table. It was the signal for his armed guards to rush into the room. Lord Stanley was wounded before he managed to escape, but Hastings was dragged from the Council chamber and down the stairs to Tower Green, where, without any trial, he was summarily executed, a log of wood serving as the block.

Three days later, the terrified Elizabeth Woodville, who had fled to Westminster for sanctuary, was persuaded to allow her younger son, the little Duke of York, to be brought to the Tower, to keep his brother company, and they were lodged together in the Garden Tower, where they were seen from time to time, playing together.

A few days later, Richard declared that his brother's marriage to Elizabeth Woodville was bigamous. This made the princes illegitimate and himself the legal heir to the throne. So it was Richard who was crowned king on that July day of 1483, amidst all the celebrations and decorations which had been prepared for Prince Edward.

The boys were seen from time to time, through the bars and windows of the Garden Tower, but gradually they appeared less and less, and within a few weeks they had disappeared for ever.

The rumour spread, and was recorded by the Mayor of London, that there was 'much whispering among the people that the King had put the children of King Edward to death'. Thirty years later Sir Thomas More collected evidence that Richard had ordered the Constable of the Tower to kill the children, and when he refused he was ordered to hand over the keys of the Tower to the sycophantic Sir James Tyrrell, who had promised Richard to arrange the matter. He employed one of the Princes' attendants, Miles Forest, and one of his own servants, John Dighton, to do the work. At midnight, these two men made their way along the curtain wall from the Lieutenant's lodgings to the Garden Tower, and gained an entrance to the upper chamber, by a doorway which has now been bricked up. They smothered the boys as they were asleep in bed. The Duke of York awoke but was quickly stilled by a dagger thrust. Tyrrell himself calmly satisfied himself that the two children were dead, and then the assassins buried them at the foot of the stairs, 'deep in the ground, under a great heap of stones'.

Nearly two hundred years later the bones of two young boys were found here, huddled together, and King Charles II ordered that they should be taken to King Henry VII's chapel at Westminster for a solemn reburial. Still there were some who said that there was no proof that these were the bones of the two little princes, but they have been examined in recent years and it has been established that they are the bones of two boys aged about ten and thirteen. Moreover, there is no reason to doubt Sir Thomas More's account, for he was a wise and truthful man. And ever after, the Garden Tower has been known as the Bloody Tower.

Jane Shore was formally accused of practising sorcery against King Richard and was brought before the Court of the Bishop of London, charged as a harlot and a witch. She was condemned to do penance in St Paul's churchyard, 'going before the cross in procession upon a Sunday with a taper in her hand', wrote Sir Thomas More, 'in which she went in countenance and face so demure, so womanly, and albeit she were out of all array save her kirtle only, yet went she so fair and lovely. . .'

Then she was committed to the Ludgate prison, but here King Richard's legal adviser, Thomas Lynon, fell in love with her and was granted permission to marry her.

She did not die in the ditch which was for ever after called Shoreditch, despite the old ballad, which ran:

> 'Thus weary of my life, at lengthe
> I yielded up my vital strength,
> Within a ditch of loathsome scent,
> Where carrion dogs did much frequent;
>
> The which now, since my dying daye,
> Is Shoreditch call'd, as writers saye;
> Which is a witness of my sinne,
> For being concubine to a king.'

Shoreditch took its name many years before Jane was born, perhaps from the family of Soerdich, who were Lords of the Manor during the fourteenth century, or from the 'soredich', which was the ditch or sewer dividing Shoreditch from Hackney. And Jane, whose marriage to Lynon was a happy one, lived on into the reign of Henry VIII.

There is an old London proverb that 'there is but one road out of the Tower, and that leads to the scaffold'. Like all generalizations of this kind, there are always exceptions. Many prisoners survived their sentences and a few escaped, but by far the greater number, particularly during Tudor times, met their end on Tower Hill, which was the main place of execution, where such men as Bishop Fisher, Sir Thomas More, Strafford and Laud met their end, while Tower Green, just west of the White Tower and in front of the Queen's

House, was reserved for the execution of the Queens Anne Boleyn and Katharine Howard, Lady Jane Grey and others very close to the Court, the Countess of Salisbury, Margaret Pole and Lady Rochford, as well as Robert Devereux, Earl of Essex.

When the saintly Bishop Fisher was executed, in his eightieth year, so weak and ill after his fourteen months of privation in the Tower that he had to be carried to the block, his head was exposed on London Bridge, on a pike, but soon strange, ethereal rays of light were seen to shine round it. After fourteen days there was no change in the face. On the contrary, each day it grew fresher and looked more alive, revealing, people said, the innocence and holiness of the blessed father. People flocked to the bridge each day to see it. Soon the crowds were so dense that carts and horses could not pass over, and by the fourteenth day the executioner was ordered, at dead of night, when nobody was about, to throw it into the river, while the body was buried in the church of St Peter ad Vincula, after resting for a time at All Hallows, Barking.

There is a tradition that Anne Boleyn spent her last night in the Queen's House (then known as the Lieutenant's Lodgings), overlooking Tower Green. Her room, very low ceilinged, was only fourteen feet square and there was a single casement window, opening on to the ramparts which extend from the top of the Bell Tower to the Beauchamp Tower.

It was only seventeen days since she had been arrested at Greenwich and taken to the Tower, insisting all the way of her innocence, and on this last night she is said to have written to the King, once more assuring him of her innocence and begging for mercy for the five men accused with her. She signed the letter 'Your most loyal and ever faithful wife' and it was claimed to have been found amongst the papers of Sir Thomas Cromwell, after his execution, but no one will ever know whether the King ever saw it, or whether it was a forgery, written some time later, in order to clear the aspersion of adultery from the mother of the Princess Elizabeth, when she became heir to the throne.

In 1864 a sentry saw Anne's ghost stealing from the Lieutenant's Lodgings, dressed in white. He challenged her but she came on towards him. Terrified, he charged with his bayonet, but as he lunged the figure disappeared and the sentry fell down in a dead faint. Here he was found by his commanding officer and was court-martialled for dereliction of duty. He told his story and fortunately for him two of his fellow sentries were able to corroborate it. They said they had been looking out of the window of the Bloody Tower and saw the woman in white gliding towards the sentry. He was believed and acquitted, and for several years after this sentries claimed to have seen the ghost, hovering between the Lodgings and Tower Green, while on moonlit nights they were ready to swear that the shadow of an axe would steal across the Green and stand erect, silhouetted against the Keep.

Sir Walter Raleigh's ghost still wanders through the cells and passages of his place of captivity in the Beauchamp Tower and on the ramparts leading to the Bell Tower, where he so often walked.

During Queen Elizabeth's reign, one of her last prisoners was Wyatt, the young Earl of Southampton. He was kept there in relative comfort and was ultimately released by King James, but there is another cat story associated with his two-year spell of imprisonment. Wyatt had a cat that was devoted to him, and disconsolate when his master left him. How the creature ever found its way to the Tower no one can say, but one day it arrived there and by some mysterious means chose the right chimney down which to climb into the Earl's cell. After that it never left him and when the time came for his release, Wyatt had his portrait painted with the faithful cat close by him, sitting on the window sill.

It was only two years after this that Guy Fawkes was committed to the Tower and put on the rack in order to try to extract a confession from him. Many years later a sentry declared that he had heard Guy's cries of agony, under torture, coming from the dungeons.

At the beginning of the Civil War, Lord Middleton was visited by a stranger, a very old man, who warned him that his party would fail and King Charles would be put to death, but that his son would ultimately be restored to the throne. Lord Middleton was taken prisoner after the battle of Worcester and sent to the Tower. Here he was visited by the ghost of his old friend Bocconi, who said he had come to reassure him that in three days' time he would escape in his wife's clothes. Then he vanished, but the prophecy came true. Lady Middleton, with the help of her maid, devised a brilliant plan of escape, and both she and Middleton got away safely to Holland.

BURIED TREASURE AT THE TOWER

After the Civil War and the establishment of the Commonwealth, the Lieutenant of the Tower was John Barkstead, one of the regicides who signed King Charles I's death warrant. When the news of the coming Restoration reached him, he is said to have buried his private hoard of money, estimated at £7,000, in one of the cellars under the Byward or Bell Tower and fled to Holland, but here he was arrested by Sir George Downing, Charles II's ambassador to the Dutch, brought back to England, and with two other regicides, hanged and quartered at Tyburn.

Pepys watched the journey to the gallows on April 19th, 1662. 'This morning, before we sat, I went to Aldgate and at the corner shop, a draper's, I stood, and did see Barkstead, Okey and Corbet drawn towards the gallows at Tiburne; and there they were hanged and quartered.'

The rumour of Barkstead's buried treasure lingered on and six months later, on October 30th, Pepys records that Lord Sandwich told him that he and Sir Harry Bennet had been told about it by Mr Wade, the story having been given to Wade by an unnamed woman, who claimed to have been a friend of Barkstead's. Lord Sandwich told him that the King's warrant ran for Pepys, on the part of Lord Sandwich, and a Mr Lee, for Sir Harry Bennet, to demand leave of the Lieutenant of the Tower to search for it. If it were found Sandwich was to have £2,000 of it, Wade £2,000 and the King £3,000. Pepys, perennially hard up, confided to his diary that he hoped for his own reward about £10 – or perhaps as much as £20.

Having gained the permission of the Lieutenant, Pepys set off for the Tower, with Wade, Lee, a guide named Evett and several porters carrying pickaxes. They lit their candles and climbed down to the cellars, hoping to find one particular arched vault. They dug in several cellars which seemed to answer the description but found nothing. At eight o'clock that night they stopped work but they tried again the following morning. Again they failed. Wade then consulted the woman who had first told him of the treasure. On November 4th Pepys wrote that Wade and Evett called at his office, 'who having been again with their prime intelligencer, a woman, I perceive; and though we have missed twice, yet they bring such an account of the probability of the truth of the thing, though we are not certain of the place, that we shall set upon it once more; and I am willing and hopeful in it. So we resolved to set upon it again on Wednesday morning; and the woman herself will be there in a disguise, and confirm us in the place.'

So on November 7th they set off once more for the Tower. 'And now privately the woman, Barkstead's great confident, is brought, who do positively say that this is the place which he did say the money was hid in, and where he and she did put up the £50,000* in butter firkins; and the very day that he went out of England did say that neither he nor his would be the better for that money, and therefore wishing that she and hers might. And so left us, and we full of hope did resolve to dig all over the cellar, which by seven o'clock at night we performed . . . But at last we saw we were mistaken; and after digging the cellar quite through, and removing the barrels from one side to the other, we were forced to pay our porters, and give over our expectations, though I do believe there must be money hid somewhere by him, or else he did delude this woman in hopes to oblige her to further serving him, which I am apt to believe.'

A week or two later, on December 19th, they decided to try once more, but it was a very cold day, so Pepys and Mr Lee spent most of the time by the fire in the Governor's house, while the workmen set to work in the garden, 'in the corner against the mayne-guard', which Pepys thought a most unlikely place anyway. They found nothing and, said Pepys,

---

*The money has mysteriously multiplied, but this is the sum now quoted in the Pepys manuscript.

'having wrought below the bottom of the foundation of the wall, I bid them to give over, and so all our hopes ended; and so went home . . .'

So whether the treasure was ever buried in the Tower or whether it is still there, whether it was £7,000 or £50,000, no one can say.

THE GHOST OF THE MARTIN TOWER

The strangest of all the stories connected with the Tower was much later than this. In 1817 Edmund Swifte was Keeper of the Crown Jewels, which at this time were kept in the Martin Tower, and Swifte and his family lived there. One Sunday night in October of that year he was having supper with his wife, her sister and their little boy. The doors were all closed and the windows covered with heavy curtains. The only light came from two candles on the table. Swifte sat at the head of the table, his son on his right, his wife on the left, facing the fire-place and his sister-in-law at the end of the table, opposite him. He offered a glass of wine to his wife and as she was about to put it to her lips, she paused and cried: 'Good God! What is it?'

'I looked up,' recorded Swifte, 'and saw a cylindrical figure like a glass tube, something about the thickness of an arm, and hovering between the ceiling and the table: its contents appeared to be a dense fluid, white and pale blue, like the gathering of a summer cloud and incessantly rolling and mingling within the cylinder. This lasted about two minutes when it began slowly moving towards my sister-in-law, following the oblong shape of the table before my son and myself. Passing behind my wife, it paused for a moment over her right shoulder. Instantly she crouched down and with both hands covering her right shoulder, shrieked out: "Oh Christ! It has seized me."

'I caught up my chair, striking at the "appearance" with a blow that hit the wainscot behind her. It then crossed the upper end of the table and disappeared in the recess of the opposite window. I rushed upstairs to the other children's room and told the terrified nurse what I had seen. Other servants hurried into the parlour, where their mistress told them the scene, even as I was detailing it above stairs.'

The following morning, after the service in the Tower church, Swifte told the Chaplain what had happened, but the Chaplain said it could only have been a delusion, particularly since neither the sister-in-law nor the son had seen anything at all: and somebody else suggested it had been a patch of mist coming from a damp chimney. But Swifte, who was a sensible, practical man, insisted that it was neither, for the apparition had actually seized his wife's shoulder.

No satisfactory answer was ever found to the mystery, and shortly afterwards there was another strange happening. A night sentry was keeping guard outside the Jewel House door. On the stroke of midnight, the figure of a huge bear appeared from under the door. The sentry struck at it with his bayonet, but as he did so the bear vanished and the bayonet stuck fast in the oak door. The man fainted and here he was found by some of his fellow sentries and carried away to the guard room.

When he recovered he told them his story and they later declared that he had not been asleep nor was he drunk. The following morning, Swifte visited him and was shocked to see the change in the man. He was trembling and still terrified, and a day or two later, still maintaining his story, he died.

THE LONDON STONE

From the Tower walk back to the City by way of Great Tower Street. The second turning on your right is Mark Lane and leading from it is Hart Street, where the little St Olave's Church and its graveyard still stand, old and placid, as though they were miles from the City, in the heart of the English countryside. St Olave's survived the Great Fire and although it was cruelly damaged during the bombing of 1941 it has been beautifully restored. It is the church where Samuel Pepys worshipped. The bust of his wife, Elizabeth, which he set up in the chancel, after her death in 1669, is still there, and both he and Elizabeth lie buried in the vault. There are no ghosts here, nor in the churchyard, but Pepys always seems very close.

Back in Great Tower Street, continue westwards along East Cheap and cross over King William Street to Cannon Street. Here, on the north side, is the Bank of China, and set in its wall is the London Stone (**6**), the origin of which is still largely a matter of conjecture amongst antiquarians.

It once stood on the south side of the street. John Stow, in the sixteenth century, wrote: 'On the south side of this high street, near unto the channel, is pitched upright a great stone, called London Stone, fixed in the ground very deep, fastened with bars of iron, and otherwise so strongly set, that if carts do run against it through negligence the wheels be broken and the stone itself unshaken. The cause why this stone was set there, the time when, or other memory is none.'

Strype, more than a century later, wrote of it: 'This stone, before the Fire of London, was much worn away, and, as it were, but a stump remaining. But it is now, for the preservation of it, cased over with a new stone, handsomely wrought, cut hollow underneath, so as the old stone may be seen, the new one being over it, to shelter and defend the old venerable one.'

In 1742 the stone was moved to the north side of Cannon Street and about fifty years later it was regarded as an obstruction and would have been destroyed, but for the intervention of a local antiquarian. It was decided to place it in the wall of St Swithin's Church, and there it remained until World War Two, when the church was so terribly damaged that it had to be demolished. The Bank of China was built on the site and the London Stone, protected by an iron grille, has been placed low down in its front wall.

It is commonly considered to be the central milestone of Roman London, similar to that in the Forum at Rome. The Roman roads of Britain radiated from this stone and it was from here that they were measured, for it was placed in the centre of the longest diameter of the second Roman London, after it was bounded by the wall, although it was on the western extremity of the first Roman London.

Some writers have suggested that it is of Saxon origin and had some religious significance, and another theory is that it may have been part of the house of Henry FitzAlwin de London Stane. He was the City of London's first mayor, holding office from 1189 until his death twenty-three years later. His house, on the site of which the first Guildhall was built, came to be known as London Stone, for it was one of the very few stone buildings in the City at this time. It has been located in Cannon Street, by St Swithin's Church, and perhaps where the third Salter's Hall stood.

This fragment of FitzAlwin's house could have been a symbol of the beginnings of independent self-government for the City, which would explain Jack Cade's boast, when he had stormed London Bridge. Striking the London Stone with his sword, he declared, 'Now is Mortimer lord of this city . . . and now henceforward it shall be treason for any that calls me other than Lord Mortimer.'

LONDON BRIDGE

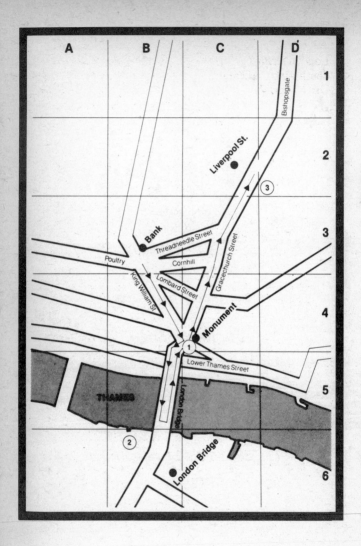

E

1 London Bridge
2 Southwark Cathedral
3 Dirty Dick's

E

BUSES
Liverpool Street: 149, 243A.
Cornhill: 15, 23, 25.
Bank: 11, 15, 21, 23, 25, 43, 76, 133, 501, 502,
London Bridge: 8A, 10, 21, 35, 40, 43, 44, 47, 48, 95, 133,
501, 513.

This is only a rough guide to the buses and you may need to consult the London Transport Bus Map.

UNDERGROUNDS
Liverpool Street
Bank
Monument
Cannon Street
London Bridge

THE ROMAN BRIDGE

There are many ways of reaching London Bridge (1), but if you are on foot in the City the simplest way is to walk down Cheapside and Poultry to the Bank of England. Cross over to King William Street, walk down to the City Monument, and you cannot fail to see the bridge, reaching over to Southwark.

This concrete bridge, built in the early 1970s, replaced the bridge built by Rennie and his sons Sir John and George Rennie, which was opened in 1832.

No one can say when the first London Bridge was built. When, in AD 43, Aulus Plautius set sail for the Kentish coast, to reduce some order between the quarrelling Celtic tribes, his army was said to have been 40,000 strong. It was composed of a mixed bag of soldiers, drawn from most of the countries of the Roman Empire. They crossed the Medway by a ford, routed the defending Belgae, and reached the Thames. The German contingent swam across, in pursuit of the fleeing Belgae, who were making for Colchester, but the rest of the soldiers – many of them engineers and craftsmen – built a bridge of rafts, close to the ford where the Walbrook stream emptied into the Thames. Here they paused to await the arrival of the Emperor Claudius, and during this time they may have built the first wooden bridge, over which the Emperor and his corps of elephants crossed, to lead the victory march into Colchester.

THE LEGEND OF JOHN OVERS

However, this does not match with the legend of old John Overs, the ferryman, which was recorded many years later, in a tract entitled 'The true History of the Life and Sudden Death of old John Overs, the rich Ferry-man of London, showing how he lost his life by his own covetousness. And of his daughter Mary, who caused the Church of St Mary Overies in Southwark to be built: and of the building of London Bridge.'

The story goes that, perhaps about the sixth or seventh century, before there was ever a bridge, there was only a ferry to carry passengers over the river from Southwark to Church-yard Alley, which was the high road between Middlesex and London. The right to employ the ferry was rented by John Overs from the City of London and he held the monopoly.

By ferrying not only foot passengers but cattle and horses, bringing farm produce to the City, he grew immensely rich, but he was a terrible old miser, as well as a usurer, and kept his servants in a miserable state of want and hunger, while his only daughter, the beautiful Mary, though more familiarly known, in later years, as Old Moll, he kept hidden away, too mean to contemplate ever paying a dowry for her marriage. Neverthe-less, Mary had a secret sweetheart, who had fallen in love with her – and perhaps her father's fortune too – when he was using the ferry one day. 'The first interview pleased well; the second better; the third concluded the match between them,' we are told.

As Overs grew richer, he grew ever meaner, and one day it occurred to him that if he pretended to be dead for twenty-four hours his household would mourn and fast, and he would save the cost of a day's food for them.

He persuaded the unhappy Mary to agree to the plan, wrapped himself in a sheet and laid himself out in his chamber, with tapers burning at his head and feet: but when the servants heard that the old skinflint was dead, far from mourning, they were overjoyed. They danced round his body, unlocked all the food stores and enjoyed the best meal of their lives.

The tract says that John bore it for as long as he was able, but when he could endure it no longer, stirring and struggling in his sheet, like a ghost with a candle in each hand, 'he purposed to rise up, and rate 'em for their sauciness and boldness; when one of them thinking that the Devil was about to rise in his likeness, being in a great amaze, catched hold of the butt-end of a broken oar, which was in the chamber, and being a sturdy knave, thinking to kill the Devil at the first blow, actually struck out his brains.'

Not only was the servant acquitted, but Overs was made an accessory of his own death and excommunicated.

When Mary's lover heard that the old man was dead and

that Mary was now not only free to marry but extremely wealthy, he hastened up from the country to claim her as his bride, but he was in such a hurry that his horse stumbled, the young man was thrown and broke his neck.

Mary was broken-hearted, but set about the mournful business of arranging her father's funeral. She found that, as he had been excommunicated, he would not be allowed a Christian burial, but at last, the friars of Bermondsey Abbey, during the absence of their Abbot, agreed that, in return for a considerable sum of money, he should be given 'a little earth for charity' in the Abbey graveyard. But when the Abbot returned, he declared that the friars had sinned against the Church by accepting money from such a man. He ordered his body to be taken up and laid on the back of his own ass, which was then to be allowed to follow its own devices and take the body to 'some place where he best deserved to be buried'. Gently the ass proceeded down Kent Street and along the highway until it came to a small pond, known as St Thomas à Waterings, by the side of which was a place of execution. The ass then shook off Overs' body, directly under the gibbet, and here it was buried.

Mary was now beset by many suitors, but she cared for none of them. Instead, she founded the priory of St Mary Overies at Southwark and spent the rest of her life there.

The nunnery was dissolved during the ninth century and a college of priests established here by St Swithun, Bishop of Winchester. During the following years it suffered many vicissitudes, but at the Dissolution, the Priory Church became the parish church, and its dedication was changed to that of St Saviour. The church was in the diocese of Rochester, but when, in 1905, the diocese was divided, and Southwark became an independent see, St Saviour's, whose history had begun with Mary Overy's nunnery , dedicated to St Mary the Virgin, became Southwark Cathedral (2).

Stow says that it was the Brothers of the College of Priests established at St Mary Overies who built the first wooden London Bridge, but this is by no means certain. There was definitely a bridge by the tenth century, for there is a record at this time of a woman, found guilty of witchcraft, who was

Southwark Cathedral.
Marianne Taylor

sentenced to be thrown over it and drowned: and by the time of King Aethelred I tolls were taken from fishing boats passing under the bridge.

But it was during the reign of Aethelred II that strange stories were told of the bridge.

LONDON BRIDGE IS FALLING DOWN

Early in the eleventh century, England was at war with the

Danish Vikings. Swein, King of Denmark, captured London and Aethelred fled to Normandy for a time, but then he formed an alliance with Olaf, who was later to become King of Norway, and together they set out to recapture the City. They sailed up the Thames and the Anglo-Saxon Chronicle records that: 'On the other side of the river there was a great market town called Southwark, and there the Danes had a great host fitted out; they had dug dikes and within they had set up a wall of trees and stones and turf, and they had a great army. King Aethelred made a mighty attack upon it, but the Danes warded it, and King Aethelred won nothing. There was a bridge over the river between the borough and Southwark, and the bridge was so broad that two wagons could be driven past each other over it. On the bridge there were built strongholds, both castles and bulwarks, down towards the stream as deep as waist-high, but under the bridge there were piles which stood down on the bed of the river.'

According to the thirteenth-century Norse sagas, it was Olaf who saved the day. Before bringing his boats up to the bridge, he covered them with thick platforms of wattle and clay, under which his men were hidden and protected, safe from the missiles which the defenders of the bridge hurled down on them. At dead of night Olaf then ordered his men to tie ropes round the timber piles of the bridge, the other ends being attached to the boats. At the next flood tide they rowed downstream again, and the ropes brought the bridge tumbling down behind them, throwing the Danish defenders into the river. The survivors fled to Southwark and London was saved again.

At the end of the saga is this poem.

'London Bridge is broken down,
Gold is won and bright renown,
Shields resounding,
War-horns sounding,
Hildur shouting in the din!
Arrows singing,
Mailcoats ringing –
Odin makes our Olaf win.'

After he became King of Norway, Olaf – or Olave, which is the English form – who was a devout Christian, was killed in a crusading war against some of his pagan subjects, and after his martyrdom and canonization, no less than six churches in London were dedicated to him, one in Southwark and five in the City of London.

In 1090, sixty years after the death of Olaf, there was a terrible storm in London and the river flooded its banks. It is said to have destroyed six hundred houses in the City, blown off the roof of Bow Church and destroyed the bridge. A second bridge was built but this was destroyed by fire.

These two disasters may have given rise to the English version of the old Norwegian verse.

> 'London Bridge is broken down,
> Dance o'er my Lady Lea
> London Bridge is broken down,
> With a gay lady.
> How shall we build it up again?'

Silver and gold will be stolen away, iron and steel will bend and bow, wood and clay will wash away, runs the jingle, but it ends triumphantly.

> 'Build it up with stone so strong,
> Dance o'er my Lady Lea
> Huzza! 'twill last for ages long,
> With a gay lady.'

Lady Lea was the river Lea, which enters the Thames just below the Pool of London. It was an important trade thoroughfare for supplies to London and at one time its mouth was heavily fortified by the Danes.

'The old Lea brags of the Danish blood,' said Drayton.

THE FIRST STONE BRIDGE

To build the bridge with stone was the right answer and the work was undertaken by Peter, the priest and chaplain of St Mary Colechurch. He began the work in 1170, the money

110

being raised by Henry II's new tax on wool, which gave rise to the story that Peter had built the arches of his bridge on wool packs. It took thirty-three years to complete and Peter did not live to see the last stages.

It was built a little to the west of the old wooden bridge and was 926 feet long and 40 feet wide, for the river was wider then than it is today. It rested on nineteen pointed arches and the piers were raised on platforms or starlings of elm tree trunks, which surrounded the base of the arches at water level, thus blocking much of the waterway. The result was that the width of water for river traffic was only about two hundred feet and it created such a powerful run of water that it poured through the narrow arches and made navigation extremely difficult.

'London Bridge was made for wise men to go over and fools to go under' ran the old proverb, for there were many accidents and drownings, and people in light craft would more often than not shore their boats at the bridge, carry them round to the other side and re-embark in calmer waters.

At the tenth pier a two-storey chapel, dedicated to St Thomas of Canterbury, was built, the lower chapel being inside the pier itself, and accessible from the river, while the upper chapel was on a level with the bridge road, and Peter was buried under the stairs which connected the two.

In 1281 there was another exceptionally severe winter. The constricted water above the bridge froze, and with the thaw great blocks of ice came hurtling down the river, causing five of the arches to give way. Yet again London Bridge had broken down, but it was duly repaired.

Houses and shops were very soon built on the bridge and the gruesome custom of displaying the dismembered heads of men who had suffered execution begun in 1305, when William Wallace's head was stuck on a long pike and fixed to the bridge. After that it was a regular custom for more than three hundred years, the last sufferer being William Stanley, a Roman Catholic goldsmith and banker, who had fallen a victim to the machinations of Titus Oates.

There is a story that early in the reign of Queen Elizabeth I some Germans who were working at the Mint, which was then in the Tower of London, became ill because of the poisonous fumes arising from the molten metal. They were told that the cure was to drink from the skull of a dead man, whereupon one of the aldermen obtained a warrant 'to take off the heads upon London Bridge and make cuppes thereof, whereof they dranke and founde some relief, though the most of them dyed'.

THE JEWS AND LONDON BRIDGE

In 1290, after years of oppression, Edward I finally expelled all the Jews from England, and it was not until the time of Cromwell that they were allowed back. It is estimated that between 15,000 and 16,000 Jews were forced to leave the country and ships were provided for them, but many were shipwrecked or robbed and thrown overboard. For safety's sake, therefore, one group, who had managed to retain enough money, hired a ship on their own account, which was to set sail just below London Bridge.

The master duly embarked on the journey with them, but after a short time he cast anchor and remained stationary until, with the ebb tide, they became beached on the sands. He thereupon invited the Jews to walk with him on dry land for a spell, until the tide changed. This they did, but the master was too quick for them. When the moment came for the turn of the tide he hurried back to the ship and re-embarked, and before the Jews could catch up with him he was on his way again. As the waters crept nearer to them and the dry patch of land grew smaller, they cried to him for help, but he told them that they ought to cry 'rather unto Moses, by whose conduct their fathers passed through the Red Sea, and therefore, if they would call to him for help, he was able enough to help them out of those raging floods, which now came upon them'.

In terror the Jews cried again and again, begging the master to save them, but he ignored them and within a few minutes they had all drowned. The master returned to the City and bragged to the King of what he had done, but what happened next is uncertain. Some say he was thanked and duly rewarded, but others affirm that he was hanged for his wickedness.

The exact spot where the tragedy is said to have happened is uncertain, but the Jewish tradition is strong that it was under London Bridge. 'The spot in the river Thames, where many of the poor exiles were drowned by the perfidy of the master-mariner, is under the influence of ceaseless rage; and however calm and serene the river is elsewhere, the place is furiously boisterous,' said a Victorian Anglo-Jewish writer. 'It is, moreover, affirmed that this relentless agitation is situated under London Bridge. There are, even at this present day, some old-fashioned Hebrew families who implicitly credit the outrageous fury of the Thames. A small boat is now and then observed . . . filled with young and old credulous Jews, steering towards the supposed spot, in order to see and hear the noisy sympathy of the waters. There are many traditions on the subject.'

THE END OF OLD LONDON BRIDGE

The bridge was to suffer many more disasters before the end. In 1437 the stone gate and tower at the Southwark end fell into the river, with two of the arches, and some fifty years later a house on the bridge collapsed and five people were drowned: but in the time of Queen Elizabeth all was restored and the magnificent Nonesuch House was built over the seventh and eighth arches. The bridge suffered a serious fire in 1632, when a number of the houses were destroyed, and several more suffered during the Great Fire of 1666. By the beginning of the eighteenth century the old bridge was in a dangerous state. The houses had run down and the shops were no longer fashionable, being mainly occupied by pin and needle makers, where 'economical ladies were accustomed to drive from the west end of the town to make cheap purchases'.

By 1760 the buildings had nearly all been cleared away, and although more attempts were made to patch up the rickety old bridge, it was at last decided that Rennie should build a new one, some hundred feet to the west, for the old one was causing at least fifty drownings a year. And when it was finally demolished, in 1832, the year that the new bridge was opened, Peter of Colechurch's bones were discovered in the old

London Bridge.
Marianne Taylor

Chapel, where they had rested for more than six hundred years. Rennie's bridge was widened in 1904 and its demolition began in 1968, when Harold King's and Charles Brown's new concrete bridge was nearing completion.

DIRTY DICK'S

There are many stories to be told of Lambeth and Bankside – the theatres – the Swan, the Globe and the Rose – the Paris Garden, with its bull- and bear-baiting, the inns – the Anchor, the Cardinal's Cap, the Falcon, the Tabard and the George – the terrible prisons – the Clink, the Marshalsea, the King's Bench and the White Lion, as well as the Stews, the rows of houses, leased from the Bishops of Winchester, where the prostitutes – the Winchester geese – plied their trade, but they are all part of history and far from legendary.

Walk back to the Monument, and this time take the right-hand fork ahead of you, which is Gracechurch Street, leading into Bishopsgate. Here, just about opposite Liverpool Street Station, you will see the famous old pub, Dirty Dick's.

114

Dirty Dick was Nathaniel Bentley, son of a prosperous hardware merchant who, when he died in 1761, left Nathaniel a wealthy young man. He became something of a dandy, dressed in the height of fashion and fell deeply in love with a beautiful girl. They adored each other and Nathaniel arranged a banquet at his house to celebrate their engagement. Everything was ready, the food and wine, the glass and silver, laid out on the dining room table, but as Nathaniel prepared a nosegay of flowers for his future bride, news reached him that she had suddenly died.

He was so grief-stricken that he thereupon ordered the dining room to be locked, and vowed that it should never be opened again during his lifetime. For the next forty years he lived the life of a recluse, unkempt and shabby. He very seldom bothered to wash and he mended his own ragged clothes. He employed a man to look after the hardware shop, and seldom appeared in it himself, although he always put up the shutters at night and took them down in the morning.

Not until he died, in 1809, was the dining room opened again. The remnants of the feast were found there, amidst the cobwebs and dust and decay, as well as the skeletons of the rats and mice which had taken the opportunity to enjoy it. Most pathetic of all were the fragments of the nosegay, which moved a visitor to write:

> 'A nosegay was laid before one special chair
> And the faded blue ribbon that bound it is there.'

However, there is a slight flaw in the story, for it seems that the Bentley shop was in Leadenhall Street, and the family owning the tavern, which came to be known as Dirty Dick's, had been in possession of it since 1745, long before the tragedy occurred. It appears that early in the nineteenth century they bought up the contents of poor Nathaniel's dining room and displayed it in their own pub, as an added attraction, to brighten up business.

FROM CHARING CROSS TO
WESTMINSTER ABBEY

Whitehall Palace

The Executioner of Charles I

Touching for the King's Evil

Royal Maundy Money

Westminster Abbey and The Legend of St Peter

The Stone of Scone

The Robbery of the Chapel of the Pyx

Buried Treasure at the Abbey

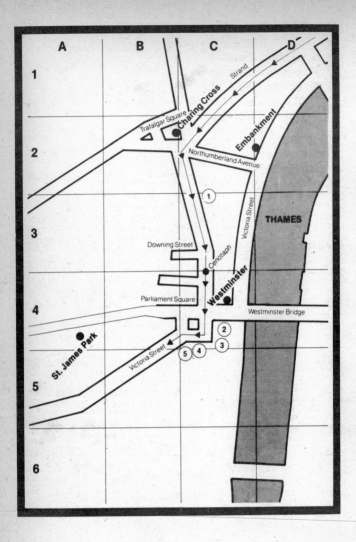

F

1 Banqueting House
2 Houses of Parliament
3 Westminster Hall
4 St Margaret's
5 Westminster Abbey

F

BUSES
Whitehall: 3, 11, 12, 24, 29, 53, 77, 77A, 77C, 88, 159, 168, 170, 172.
Strand: 1, 6, 9, 11, 13, 15, 77, 77A, 77C, 168, 170, 172, 176.
Westminster Bridge: 12, 53, 70, 76, 77C, 109, 155, 159, 170, 172, 184, 503.
Millbank: 3, 77, 77A, 159, 168.
Victoria Street: 11, 24, 29, 70, 76, 503.

This is only a rough guide to the buses and you may need to consult the London Transport Bus Map.

UNDERGROUNDS
Westminster
Charing Cross
Embankment
St James' Park

WHITEHALL PALACE

From Charing Cross, walk down the east side of Whitehall. The Thames makes a sharp bend here, so you will be walking parallel with the river, and you are covering the ground over which the great, sprawling palace of Whitehall once stretched.

There had been a mansion on this site, by the river, for centuries, and when it came into the possession of the Bishops of York, it was known as York House. When it passed to the Lord Cardinal of York, Thomas Wolsey, at the height of his enormous wealth and power, he rebuilt the old place and filled it with glittering treasures of gold and silver plate, tapestries, jewels and furniture, fit only, thought Henry VIII, for a King.

Wolsey fell from grace and departed ignominiously from the water steps of York House. Little more than a year later, he was dead, and King Henry moved, with Anne Boleyn, from the damp and dilapidated medieval Palace of Westminster, into York House, changing its name to the Whitehall Palace. The King enlarged the place until it became a labyrinth of gorgeously appointed State apartments, private dwellings for members of the Court, public offices, strange, secret passages, courtyards and gardens, covering twenty-four acres: and across the roadway, where the present Whitehall runs, were built two massive gateways, the Holbein Gate at one end, designed by Holbein, who, as Court painter, had apartments in the Palace, and the King's Gate at the other, marking the boundaries of the Palace precincts.

James I had little liking for the place and wanted Inigo Jones to rebuild it, but the plans never went beyond the building of the beautiful banqueting house, which was almost the only part to survive the fire of 1698. And Mary of Modena, James II's second wife, declared it to be the largest and most uncomfortable house in the world.

As you walk down Whitehall, the first indication of its past Royal residents is Great Scotland Yard, which was once the part of the palace reserved for Scottish visitors and their retinues, the last being Henry VIII's sister Margaret, widow of James IV of Scotland, who lived there for a time, but after her death this part of the palace was not used again. It fell into ruins and was eventually demolished.

Walk on a few yards and on the far corner of the Horse Guards Avenue is the Banqueting House (1), with its magnificent domed ceiling, painted by Rubens. It was Charles I who commissioned this work and it was from this room that he stepped to his execution in Whitehall, on January 30th, 1649.

THE EXECUTIONER OF CHARLES I

The night before the execution, the King had been lodged, under guard, at St James' Palace. He rose before 8 o'clock on that bitterly cold morning and is said to have put on an extra shirt, lest he shivered in the icy wind, and the watching crowds might think he trembled from fear. He took Communion, and at 10 o'clock was escorted, on foot, across St James' Park and up to the first floor of the Holbein Gate. Passing over the passage way of the gate, above the heads of the waiting crowds and the black-draped scaffold, which had been set up at the palace entrance, he was taken to his private apartments, to await the final summons, which came two hours later.

Then he was escorted through the banqueting house, and from one of its windows, probably the staircase window, stepped on to the scaffold, where two masked executioners awaited him, while the people in their thousands watched in silence, many in tears for the 'saddest sight that England ever saw.'

But who struck the fatal blow? That was the question that was asked at the Restoration and was never satisfactorily answered. One of the sheriff's officers declared that it was a Richard Brandon, who lived in Rosemary Lane. Within an hour of the execution he received forty shillings for his work and from the King's pocket obtained an orange stuck with cloves and a pocket handkerchief. In Whitehall he was offered twenty shillings for these relics but refused to part with them, yet back in Rosemary Lane he accepted only ten shillings for them.

Brandon survived the execution for less than six months, for on June 21st he died and was buried at St Mary's Church, Whitechapel: and a note was added to the burial register: 'This R. Brandon is supposed to have cut off the head of Charles the First.'

Yet several other names were suggested, including a man named Peachall, who died in America in 1670 and confessed on his death bed that he had been paid £100 for the execution, but afterwards was ostracized by his friends and neighbours and forced to leave the country.

Another man, a cattle drover from St Ives, made a death bed confession that he had been sent for by Oliver Cromwell, at the end of 1648, to do the deed, and had lived under an assumed name ever since.

Among Archbishop Tenison's papers at Lambeth, a letter dated October 30th, 1696 was found, saying that when King Charles came out on to the scaffold, he told Bishop Juxon that he could tell by the man's hands that one of the masked executioners was Grey of Groby, son of the Earl of Stamford.

Anthony à Wood said it was Thomas Trappen, the surgeon who had been present with Cromwell at the battle of Worcester.

Yet the final opinion was that Richard Brandon was probably the executioner, with Grey as his assistant. In fact he is said to have made a confession, declaring that when he was first approached, he refused, declaring that he would rather be put to death himself than do it; but later he was 'fetched out of bed by a troop of horse and compelled to perform the dreadful deed'.

A few days after his death, a pamphlet was published, claiming to be 'The Confession of Richard Brandon the Hangman upon his Death Bed, concerning his beheading his late Majesty Charles the First, King of Great Britain and his Protestation and Vow touching the same; the manner how he was terrified in conscience, the Apparitions and Visions which appeared unto him; the great judgment that befell him three days before he dy'd; and the manner how he was caryed to White-Chappell Churchyard on Thursday night last, the Strange Actions that happened thereupon.'

Brandon is made to declare that he no sooner stepped on to the scaffold than he 'fell a trembling and hath ever since continued in the like agony'. And there was a report that, at his funeral, a vast crowd of people stood waiting to see his corpse carried into the churchyard, cursing and reviling him for executing the King and crying 'Hang him, Rogue. Bury him in the Dunghill.'

Many English men and women were appalled at the sentence passed on the sad, misguided little King and several old country folk, who understood little of the causes of the Civil War and had been unaffected by it, are said to have died of grief and shock when the news reached them, for, like Charles himself, they believed implicitly that the King's person was holy and his appointment divine.

TOUCHING FOR THE KING'S EVIL

It was at the palace of Whitehall, particularly during Stuart times, that the ceremony of touching for the King's Evil was performed.

The King's Evil was the disease of scrofula, and as early as the time of Edward the Confessor it was believed that it could be cured by the touch of the King, who possessed the divine hereditary right to serve his people in this way.

But the custom is even earlier, for the French Kings laid claim to this divine power in the fifth century. In England, Peter de Blois refers to the custom in the twelfth century, so it is probable that it continued during the reigns of the Norman and Plantagenet kings, although there is no direct evidence for this: but during the Wars of the Roses, Sir John Fortescue, the distinguished judge, in defending the claim of the House of Lancaster to the throne, argued that the crown could not descend to a woman, 'because the queen is not qualified, by the terms of her anointing at the coronation, to cure the disease called "the King's Evil" '.

The practice was continued by the Tudors, and Henry VII introduced the custom of presenting each victim brought to him with a small gold or silver coin, called a touch-piece, as he said the magic words: 'I touch, but God healeth': but it became most popular with the advent of the Stuarts.

At this time advertisements were placed in the gazettes, announcing when and where the King would be curing his subjects of scrofula with the touch of the royal hand, and most frequently it was at Whitehall Palace. Here, for example, is a notice issued, by order of King Charles I, from Whitehall Palace on May 16th, 1644.

'His Sacred Majesty having declared it to be his Royal will and purpose to continue the healing of his people for the Evil during the month of May and then to give over till Michaelmas next, I am commanded to give notice thereof, that the people may not come up to town in the interim, and lose their labour.'

There is no record of the numbers who were actually cured of the disease after the ceremony, but there were no doubt many cases of faith healing. As an added precaution, sufferers were recommended to wear round their necks, in little silk bags, pieces of verbena root, which had sacred properties. Alternatively, and more prosaically, baked toads were advised, which takes us back again to the fifth century, for the device of Clovis was three toads, which were believed to have magically protective powers.

'My Lord Anglesey had a daughter cured of the King's Evil with three others on Tuesday,' wrote William Greenhill to Lady Bacon, in December of 1629.

There is a vivid account of one of these cures in the manuscript diary of Oudert. 'A young gentlewoman, Elizabeth Stephens, of the age of sixteen, came to the Presence Chamber in 1640, to be "touched for the Evil", with which she was so afflicted that, by her own and her mother's testimony, she had not seen with her left eye for above a month. After prayers read by Dr Sanderson, she knelt down to be "touched" with the rest by the King. His Majesty then touched her in the usual manner, and put a ribbon with a piece of money hanging to it about her neck. Which done, his Majesty turned to the Duke of Richmond, the Earl of Southampton, and the Earl of Lindsay, to discourse with them. And the young gentlewoman said of her own accord, openly, "Now God be praised, I can see of this sore eye," and afterwards that she did see more and more by it, and could by degrees endure the light of a candle.'

Charles II touched for the Evil before his Restoration, during his years of exile in France and the Netherlands. Sir William Lower recorded, in his *Relation of the Voyage and Residence which Charles II Hath Made in Holland*, published in 1660, that 'It is certain that the King hath very often touched the sick, as well at Breda, where he touched 260 from Saturday the 17 of April to Sunday the 23 of May, as at Bruges and Bruxels, during the residence that he made there; and the English assure . . .it was not without success, since it was the experience that drew thither every day, a great number of those diseased, even from the most remote provinces of Germany.'

During the first four years of his restoration King Charles is said to have touched nearly twenty-four thousand people, and the total number until the year before his death was estimated at 92,107. In that year, 1684, more than ever came to be cured, and in the jostling crowds some are said to have been trampled to death. By that time the ceremony had become more elaborate and the 'Office for the Healing' was included in the book of Common Prayer.

The King, on his chair of state, under a rich canopy, sat in the great hall of the palace. Each surgeon led his patients in turn to the foot of the throne. As a chaplain spoke the words 'He put His hands upon them and healed them', the King stroked the face of each sufferer with both his hands, and when they had all been touched in this way, they came up to the throne again, in the same order, and the King hung round the neck of each a blue ribbon, on which was threaded a gold coin – an angel – for it bore the impression of St Michael the Archangel on one side and a ship in full sail on the other – and was of the value of ten shillings. During this part of the ceremony the chaplain chanted, 'This is the true Light who came into the world,' and the ceremony ended with the reading of the epistle for the day and prayers for the sick.

On June 23rd 1660 Samuel Pepys, happening to be at White-hall on other matters, 'staid to see the King touch people for the King's evil. But he did not come at all, it rayned so; and the poor people were forced to stand all the morning in the rain in the garden. Afterwards he touched them in the Banqueting-house'.

Later that year, at the beginning of November, Mr Holliard, a surgeon at St Thomas's Hospital, called to see Pepys and stayed to dinner. They talked about the cure for the King's Evil, but Mr Holliard, being a man of science, was an avowed sceptic. 'He do deny altogether any effect at all,' wrote Pepys.

In April of the following year, when Pepys saw the ceremony for himself, he said that it seemed to him to be 'an ugly office and a simple one'.

James II continued the practice, and although William of Orange scorned to have any part in it, it was revived by Queen Anne. By this time, since most of the Whitehall Palace had been destroyed by fire, the ceremony was held at St James's Palace, and the numbers seem to have been as great as in the time of her uncle, Charles II.

On March 30th, 1712, the newspapers recorded that the Queen had touched two hundred sufferers, and on this occasion one of the 'touched' was Samuel Johnson, then a child of two, whose mother declared that he had contracted the disease from a nursemaid. 'His mother,' says Boswell, 'yielding to the superstitious notion, which it is wonderful to think, prevailed so long in this country, as to the virtue of the regal touch; a notion which our kings encouraged. . .carried him to London, where he was actually touched by Queen Anne. Mrs Johnson, indeed, as Mr Hector informed me, acted by the advice of the celebrated Sir John Flower, then a physician at Lichfield.'

When Johnson was asked whether he could remember Queen Anne, he said he had a 'confused but somehow a sort of solemn recollection of a lady in diamonds, and a long black hood'. But sadly Boswell adds that the touch was without any effect.

Although for some years after the accession of the Hanoverians, the Office for the Healing was still included in the prayer book, the custom of touching for the Evil seems to have ended with the death of Queen Anne, but for long afterwards the coins which had been touched by the monarch were regarded as having the power to ward off evils of all kinds, and the Pretender Charles Edward Stuart had his own touch-pieces made, for with his assumption of the right to the English crown, he also asserted that he possessed the power to confer royal cures.

ROYAL MAUNDY MONEY

Another ceremony that took place in the Whitehall Palace

during the reign of Charles II was the distribution of the Royal Maundy money, on Maundy Thursday, the day before Good Friday. This was in commemoration of Christ's mandate on that day, after he had washed the disciples' feet, when He said to them 'a new commandment give I unto you, that ye love one another', adding 'I have given you an example that ye should do as I have done to you'.

This ancient ceremony was performed in most countries of Christendom in medieval times, and among the records we learn that, about the year 1300, the abbot of Westminster sat in the east cloister on Maundy Thursday and washed the feet of thirteen poor men, after which, having dried them with a towel and kissed them, he gave them money, food and beer.

The custom was observed in parish churches throughout the country until, in time, the monarch replaced the representatives of the Church. It was Henry IV who began the practice of relating the number of recipients to the age of the sovereign, so that it increased each year. At one time they had to be of the same sex as the sovereign, but by the eighteenth century an equal number of men and women were chosen.

How the choice was made is not clear, but presumably they were recommended by their parish priests, as being in need.

In 1661 Charles II washed the feet of thirty-one of his poor subjects in the Great Hall in the Whitehall Palace. At the same time he gave every man a purse of white leather, containing thirty-one pence, and a red purse in which was a piece of gold. They were also given a shirt, a suit of clothes, shoes and stockings, a wooden dish, and a basket containing four loaves, half a salmon, a whole ling, twelve red herrings and twelve white herrings. After this they had a drink of claret, a service was conducted in the King's chapel and they all departed, saying 'God save the King!'.

By 1667 Pepys was recording that 'the King did not wash the poor people's feet himself, but the Bishop of London did it for him', James II was the last monarch to wash the people's feet himself and after that time the ceremony was performed by the Royal Almoner and became increasingly elaborate. The Banqueting Hall had become the Chapel Royal, though it was never consecrated, and in 1731, when George II was on the throne, 'it being Maundy Thursday, the King being then in his forty-eighth year, there was distributed at the Banqueting House, Whitehall, to forty-eight poor men and forty-eight poor women, boiled beef and shoulders of mutton, and small bowls of ale, which is called dinner; after that, large wooden platters of fish and loaves, viz undressed, one large ling and one dried cod; twelve red herrings and twelve white herrings, and four half-quartern loaves. Each person had one platter of this provision; after which was distributed to them shoes, stockings, linen and woollen cloth, and leathern bags, with one penny, twopenny, threepenny and fourpenny pieces of silver, and shillings, to each about four pounds in value. His Grace the Lord Archbishop of York, Lord High Almoner, also performed the annual ceremony of washing the feet of the poor in the Royal Chapel, Whitehall, as was formerly done by the kings themselves'.

The feet washing was discontinued in 1737 and gradually the form of the ceremony changed. On Maundy Thursday of 1814, during the Regency, it was recorded that 'In the morning the Sub-Almoner, the Secretary of the Lord High Almoner, and others belonging to the Lord Chamberlain's office, attended by a party of the Yeomen of the Guard, distributed to seventy-five poor women and seventy-five poor men, being as many as the King was years old, a quantity of salt fish, consisting of salmon, cod and herrings, pieces of very fine beef, five loaves of bread, and some ale to drink the King's health. . . A procession entered of those engaged in the cermony, consisting of a party of the Yeomen of the Guard, one of them carrying on his head a large gold dish, containing one hundred and fifty bags with seventy-five silver pennies in each, for the poor people, which was placed in the royal closet. They were followed by the Sub-Almoner, in his robes, with a sash of fine linen over his shoulder and crossing his waist. It was followed by two boys, two girls, the secretary, and other gentlemen, all carrying nosegays. The Church Evening Service was then performed, at the conclusion of which the silver pennies were distributed, and woollen cloth, linen, shoes and stockings, to the men and women, and a cup of wine to drink the King's health.'

During the nineteenth century the ceremony was greatly simplified and the distribution of food ceased altogether, but the Maundy money was still given. Until 1891, it was still presented at the Banqueting House, but in that year Queen Victoria granted the building to the Royal United Services Institution, and the Maundy Money was once more distributed at Westminster Abbey (5), by the Sovereign, attended by the Lord High Almoner.

Today the ceremony is still held. Many of the old traditions are maintained, but the recipients are now men and women, over 65 years of age, who are chosen by their clergy for the Christian service they have given to the Church and community: and the ceremony is held only about once in four years in London, in other years taking place in cities and towns throughout the country, from which the recipients have been chosen. They are no longer poor and needy and the gifts they receive are symbolic.

During the ceremony the women are handed green purses, the men white ones, each containing money in place of the clothing once distributed. Later in the service, another distribution is made, when they are each handed a red purse and a white purse, the red one containing money in lieu of

Houses of Parliament.
Marianne Taylor

provisions and the white one the Maundy silver pennies, two-pences, threepences and fourpences, amounting to as many pence as the years of the Sovereign's age.

They are legal tender, the value of a set of Maundy coins being now ten new pence. It is a great honour to receive them and they are greatly treasured.

WESTMINSTER ABBEY AND THE LEGEND OF ST PETER

Walk down Whitehall, past all the government offices, the Cenotaph and Downing Street, and you reach Parliament Square, with St Margaret's (4) and Westminster Abbey (5) on the far side. On your left is Westminster Bridge and just above it the Houses of Parliament (2), while beyond them is all that is left of the Old Palace, the magnificent, medieval Great Hall (3).

St Margaret's Westminster with Big Ben behind.
Marianne Taylor

St Margaret's is the mother church of the City of Westminster and since 1614 it has been the parish church of the House of Commons. It is a very old foundation, dating from Saxon times, when Edward the Confessor built the first church here, dedicated to St Margaret of Antioch.

Westminster Abbey claims an even older history. There is a legend that there was once a temple of Apollo on this site, just as people talked of a temple of Diana on the site of St Paul's, but there is no evidence at all for either story, even though the monks of Westminster told of the ancient temple of Apollo having been destroyed by an earthquake.

The site of the Abbey was known as Thorney Island – a patch of dry ground rising from the marshy banks of the Thames, where it was joined by the Tyburn stream – and here, in the late sixth century, Sebert, King of the East Saxons, who had been converted to Christianity by the missionaries of St Augustine, built his first church. It was dedicated to St Peter and consecrated by Mellitus, the first Bishop of London.

There is a legend that on the night before the consecration St Peter himself appeared on the Surrey side of the river and asked a fisherman to row him across to the north bank. This the fisherman did, and as he watched his unknown passenger enter Sebert's new church, it suddenly glowed with a brilliance which lit up the night sky, and the air was filled with the singing of angels.

St Peter then wrote on the pavement of the church the Greek and Hebrew alphabet, anointed the walls with holy oil, lit the taper and sprinkled the holy water. He had dedicated his own church.

He then told the ferryman to describe to Mellitus all he had seen, and promised him that when he next went fishing, he would catch a miraculous draught, which would mostly be salmon. He also said that he and his fellow fishermen would never lack for fish, provided they gave one-tenth of their catch to the newly consecrated church, and never fished on Sundays.

It was nearly five hundred years after this that Edward the Confessor, who had rebuilt the ancient Palace of Westminster, after it had been destroyed by fire, also rebuilt the minster of St Peter, which had by this time become established as a

Benedictine monastery, with an endowment for the support of twelve monks. The Confessor died and was buried before the high altar of his new Abbey church, only a few days after its consecration. A week or two later, Harold, the last of the Saxon kings was crowned there, but before the year was out, it saw the coronation of his successor, William I. And from that Christmas day of 1066, St Peter's Abbey has been the coronation place of nearly every English sovereign.

Through early medieval times, the tradition of the fishermen and the salmon continued and the monks received their share, although with the passing of time it was less willingly yielded. Nevertheless, as late as 1382, there is a story of a Thames fisherman who brought in a large salmon for St Peter. It was carried through the refectory, and the Prior and the whole fraternity rose, as it passed up to the high table. And when it had been formally received, in the name of St Peter, the fisherman was given ale and bread from the cellarer, for his devotion.

THE STONE OF SCONE

It was Edward I who brought back from his Scottish war the stone of Scone, which to this day rests under the seat of the coronation throne in the Abbey. Legend says it was the stone on which the kings of Tara were installed, on the hill of Tara. It was taken away by Fergus, son of Eric, to Argyllshire, and from there, in the ninth century, King Kenneth took it to Scone, where it was enclosed in a wooden chair, on which the Scottish kings were henceforth crowned. Edward I brought both the chair and the stone to London in 1297, and when the Scots demanded their return, as well as most of the Scottish regalia, he sent back the chair but not the stone, for he considered it too precious ever to part with, it being, they said, the pillow on which Jacob had slept all night, when he was on the road to Padan, fleeing from the wrath of his brother Isaac. Here he dreamt that he saw a ladder 'set up on the earth, and the top of it reached to heaven: and behold the angels of God ascending and descending on it'. And God said to Jacob 'the land whereon thou liest, to thee will I give it, and to thy seed'.

Westminster Abbey, Chapel of the Pyx.
British Tourist Authority

The stone of Scone had become particularly dear to the Scots, for there was another legend which said that 'wherever this stone is round, there will reign some of the Scotch race of Kings'; and the bitter resentment at its loss, lingered on for many a year. Nevertheless Edward I had a coronation chair especially made to hold the stone, and in this chair almost every succeeding English monarch has been crowned.

THE ROBBERY OF THE CHAPEL OF THE PYX

Only six years later, in 1303, retribution came to Edward I. He kept his private treasure, as well as much of the wealth he had accumulated during the Scottish wars, in the Chapel of the Pyx. This you can easily find, by passing through the door in the south choir aisle, just below the south transept, which leads into the cloisters. These are small and intimate and very old, the simple thirteenth and fourteenth-century arcades surrounding a small lawn.

From the east walk is a door giving on to a dark, vaulted vestibule, which leads to the Chapter House: and close by, just beyond the entrance to the library and muniment room, is the Chapel of the Pyx, an ancient, vaulted chamber where, for many years, the treasury of England was to be kept, as well as the Pyx, which was a box containing standard pieces of coinage, against which current gold and silver coins were, from time to time, tested.

In Edward I's time, the Chapel had double doors and was made secure with seven huge locks, yet they were forced and a vast amount of treasure was stolen. Suspicion at once fell on the Abbot and his monks. King Edward was at Linlithgow when the news reached him, and although most of them were afterwards released, he immediately sent orders down to London for the arrest of the Abbot, forty-eight of the monks and some thirty-two other men, all of whom were committed to the Tower.

John de Drokensford, Master of the King's Wardrobe, went forthwith to the Abbey to investigate. He 'opened the doors of the Treasury, and entered therein with the company assembled, and he found the Treasury broken into, the chests and coffers broken open, and many goods carried away', but the King's crown and three other crowns, which would have been easily recognizable when it came to disposing of them, had been left behind, strewn carelessly and hurriedly about the floor.

Evidence of the thieves soon came to light, for although knavery was no doubt as frequent in medieval times as it is today, it seems to have been considerably less efficient in its execution, the rascals relying too confidently on the naivety of their victims.

William the Palmer, Keeper of the King's Palace, said that he saw the Sacrist of the Abbey, the Sub-Prior and various monks go in and out, early and late, about the time of the burglary, and they often carried many things towards the church, what things he knew not.

On a certain day the monk Alexander of Pershore and others of his brethren were seen to take a boat and row from the Abbey out upon the Thames, loading it with two large panniers covered with black leather, in which there was a great weight – of treasure, no doubt – although William Palmer, who was himself suspected of complicity, professed not to know this. All he would say was that they returned late, after the evening bell, in another boat.

Five other robbers took more treasure away on horseback, for two nights running. In the City records in the Guildhall, there is an account of the movements of William de Kinebautone and his brother John, together with Chastanea la Bahere and her sister Alice, who met that week in a house within the close of Fleet prison, 'together with a horseman and five other ribalds, unknown, for two nights, and there spent the time until midnight eating and drinking, and then withdrew with arms towards Westminster. In the morning they returned and this they did for two nights'.

When this story was heard, they became strong suspects and the City's officers and King's marshals were ordered to take them, dead or alive, but they were never seen or heard of again.

It was discovered that, with the connivance of some of the monks, John de Linton had sown tall-growing flax in the cloister garden, and when the time came for it to be reaped, refused to allow it to be disturbed. It provided an excellent hiding place for the treasure, only five yards from the Pyx, until it could be dispersed, but within a few days much of it had been sold.

A travelling merchant for wool, cheese and butter took some of it, selling items in Northampton and then in Colchester, but when he was seized he still had a good deal in his possession. He was tortured until he confessed and informed on his accomplices. He said he had been the instigator of the robbery and that a certain John Allon had made the tools for the break-in.

John de Ramage was suspected, because he was seen coming and going from the Abbey and suddenly 'dressed very richly and acquired horses and arms'. And like many a simple-minded criminal since, he boasted that he could 'buy a town if he pleased!'

Some of the treasure was found in the cell of Richard de Podelicote himself, the Sacrist of the Abbey, who was already under suspicion, but when he was accused, he talked his way out of the trouble by saying that he had found the articles, and not knowing how they had come to be outside the Chapel, had put them in his cell for safe-keeping. He was released, but the rest of the culprits went to the gallows. Yet, to this day, no one can be certain which of the monks of the Abbey were implicated.

After this, an additional door was added to the Chapel of the Pyx, blocking the passage which led to the monks' dormitory: and the door was said to have been covered with the skin of the thieves, as a warning to future miscreants. For years afterwards stains on the door were said to be fragments of human skin.

BURIED TREASURE AT THE ABBEY

There is an even stranger story to tell of the Abbey. In 1634, during the reign of Charles I, David Ramsay, the King's clock-maker, was told, in great secrecy, that a large quantity of treasure was buried in the Abbey cloisters. He passed the information on to the Dean, who gave him permission to search for it, provided a due share was given to the Abbey.

Ramsay consulted John Scott of Pudding Lane, who was skilled in the use of divining rods, and William Lilly, the astrologer, joined them, Lilly being the man who had learnt his art from Evans, a drunken, unfrocked rogue of a parson, who told fortunes in Gunpowder Alley, off Fleet Street, and who, according to his pupil, was 'seldom without a black eye'.

It was a dark, quiet winter's night when, with one or two workmen and a few onlookers, who had heard what was afoot, they entered the cloisters. On the west side, the rods turned, and their hopes rose. The workmen dug down for about six feet and came across a coffin, but it was very light and promised nothing, so they did not open it. They moved into the Abbey Church. Immediately there sprang up a terrible storm of wind, loud and blustering. The rods would not move. The candles and torches burnt dimly. Some went out

Interior of Westminster Abbey.
British Tourist Authority

altogether. The wind howled louder than ever and they thought that the west end of the church was about to collapse.

'John Scott, my partner, was amazed, looked pale, knew not what to think or do,' wrote Lilly in his autobiography, 'until I gave directions and command to dismiss the demons, which when done all was quiet again, and each man returned unto his lodging late, about twelve o'clock at night. I could never since be induced to join with any in such like actions.

'The true miscarriage of the business was by reason of so many people being present at the operation, for there were about thirty – some laughing, others deriding us; so that if we had not dismissed the demons, I believe most part of the abbey church had been blown down. Secrecy and intelligent operators, with a strong confidence and knowledge of what they are doing, are best for this work.'

So the treasure was never found, but the faith in Lilly's occult powers was not diminished, except by the few sceptics. Just as a century earlier the necromancer, Dr Dee, had been invited by Lord Dudley to consult the stars and the spirit world, in order to choose the time most propitious for the coronation of Queen Elizabeth, so Lilly was consulted by Royalists, on behalf of King Charles. He was asked to name the most favourable day and hour for the King's attempted escape from Carisbrooke Castle. Unfortunately for the King and his friends, Lilly had become a Parliament spy, and the escape plot failed. General Fairfax had great faith in the man and during the siege of Colchester sent for him to put new heart into his soldiers. Yet at the Restoration, Lilly was loud in his condemnation of Cornet Joyce, who, he said, had betrayed King Charles, when he induced him to leave Holmby House and be taken to Hampton Court.

For thirty-six years he published an almanac, full of cabalistic signs and mysteries, foretelling the coming year's events, as Old Moore was to do after him, and in 1666, after the Great Fire, he was sent for by Parliament, to explain one of his signs, which purported to foretell the disaster: and he no doubt bemused all but the most hardened unbelievers with the obscure sophistry of his answer.

FROM THE BRITISH MUSEUM TO HIGHGATE

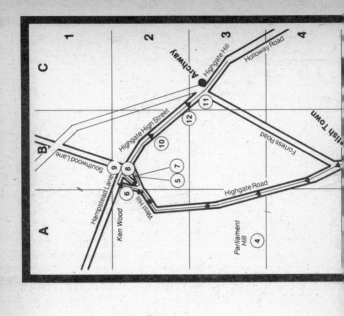

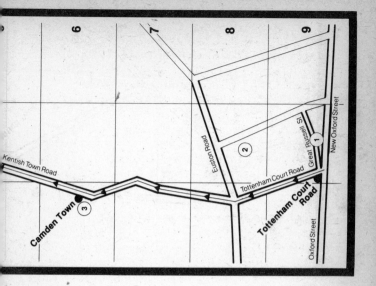

G

G

BUSES
Tottenham Court Road to Camden Town: 24, 29, 134.
Camden Town to Kentish Town: 27, 134, 137, 214.
Highgate Road to Parliament Hill Fields: 214.
Highgate High Street to Archway: 143, 210, 271.
Archway: 27, 41, 45, 137, 143, 172, 239, 263.

This is only a rough guide to the buses and you may need to consult the London Transport Bus Map.

UNDERGROUNDS
Tottenham Court Road
Camden Town
Kentish Town
Archway

MONTAGU HOUSE

The nearest tube station to the British Museum is Tottenham Court Road, which is on both the Northern and Central Lines. From the station, walk a few yards down Tottenham Court Road, past the Dominion cinema, and take the first turning on your right, which is Great Russell Street. The British Museum (1) is not five minutes' walk away, on your left.

On this site once stood Montagu House, the home of Lord Ralph Montagu, who was to become the first Duke. The first house was destroyed by fire in 1686, only eleven years after it had been built, and the loss was estimated at more than £40,000, but work on the second house began almost at once. There is a story that Lord Montagu acquired the money by a judicious marriage with the widowed Duchess of Albemarle. The young Duke of Albemarle had bought Clarendon House in Piccadilly from the Clarendon family, but soon ran through the fortune he had inherited from his father, so he sold the house to a syndicate of building developers and went off to Jamaica, ostensibly as Governor, but mainly to look for the treasure of a Spanish galleon, which had sunk near the island. He and his party of treasure seekers found it, but shortly afterwards the Duke died, being a hard drinker and 'burnt to a cinder with hot liquor'. Hans Sloane, then a young man, had gone to Jamaica with the Duke, as his physician, and he now proceeded to accompany the widowed Duchess back to England, bringing with him his first specimens of tropical fauna and flora, but on the voyage the alligator died, the iguana jumped overboard and the snake, escaping from its jar, was shot by the Duchess's terrified footman. Worse than all this, the Duchess, who had always been eccentric, went off her head. She had cheated the Duke's partners of their share of the Spanish treasure and brought it all back to England with her, so she was now a very rich woman: and despite the disability of her mental state, she was not lacking in suitors impecunious enough to appreciate her wealth rather than her person. But by now she was so mad that she declared she would marry no one but the Emperor of China. Ralph Montagu overcame this difficulty by assuring her that he himself was none other than the Emperor, and she duly married him, whereupon he took the treasure, locked her up for the rest of her life, and built the second Montagu House: and here, nearly a century later, when the house had fallen empty, the first collection of the British Museum, largely that of Hans Sloane, was housed, until Smirke's new museum was built on the site.

THE CAPPER SISTERS

In the early eighteenth century there was little building in Bloomsbury apart from the two great mansions Montagu House and Bedford House, whose gardens joined, and Thanet House, and behind them to the north was a stretch of farmlands, fields and marshes, rising to the hills of Hampstead and Highgate.

Behind Montagu House was a farm of some hundred acres, which the Capper sisters had inherited from their father. They were two fierce old spinsters, who always wore riding habits and men's hats, and they guarded their property against trespassers with a relentless fury. . .'one rode an old grey mare, and it was her spiteful delight to ride with a large pair of shears after boys who were flying their kites, purposely to cut their strings', recorded J T Smith, in his *Book For A Rainy Day*, while the other sister busied herself taking possession of the clothes of the boys who dared to bathe in their stream.

THE FIELD OF THE FORTY FOOTSTEPS

To the north of their farm, as far as where the Euston Road now runs, was a marshy, desolate stretch of countryside, yielding nothing but watercress beds, and during the seventeenth and eighteenth centuries it was often used as a duelling ground, the most famous duel of all being that fought in 1685 between two brothers, who had fallen in love with the same girl. She found it impossible to choose between them, so they decided to fight for her. She went with them to the field and sat calmly by, while the young men fought with such bitterness that they killed each other. Their footsteps remained indented in the ground, and ever after no vegetation would grow over them, whereupon the ground became known as the Field of the Forty Footsteps (2), a place of haunting and magic, notwithstanding the prosaic observation of J T Smith that, with the passing years, the footsteps were so often trodden over by sightseers, that nothing could have grown there anyway.

Many years later, Robert Southey went to explore the spot. 'We sought for nearly half an hour in vain,' he said. 'We could find no steps within a quarter of a mile, no, nor half a mile, of Montagu House. We were almost out of hope, when an honest man who was at work, directed us to the next ground, adjoining to a pond. There we found what we sought, about three-quarters of a mile north of Montagu House, and 500 yards east of Tottenham Court Road. The steps are of the size of a human foot, about three inches deep, and lie from north-east to south-west. We counted only seventy-six; but we were not exact in our counting. The place where one or both the brothers are supposed to have fallen, is still bare of grass. The labourer also showed us the bank where (the tradition is) the wretched woman sat to see the combat.'

This is puzzling, for the tradition is that there were only forty footsteps, yet the brothers must have taken considerably more steps than this during their fight, but we shall never know, for by the early years of the nineteenth century the field had disappeared under the new buildings of Bloomsbury.

There is another legend attached to this place. In 1694, less than ten years after the tragedy of the two brothers, Aubrey wrote: 'The last summer, on the day of St John Baptist (mid-summer day), I accidentally was walking in the pasture behind Montagu House: it was twelve o'clock. I saw there about two or three and twenty young women, most of them well habited, on their knees very busied, as if they had been weeding. I could not presently learn what the matter was; at last a young man told me, that they were looking for a coal under the root of a plantain to put under their heads that night, and they should dream who would be their husband. It was to be found that day and hour.'

MOTHER RED CAP OF CAMDEN TOWN

It is a dreary walk to Camden Town, and the simplest way to reach it is to return to Tottenham Court Road tube station and take the Northern Line, for it is only five stations away.

Here, close to the station, is the Old Mother Red Cap (**3**): and a tavern has stood on this site for more than two hundred and fifty years. Jinny, the first Mother Red Cap, more often known as Mother Damnable, was born early in the seventeenth century, the only child of a brick maker, Jacob Bingham. When she was fifteen, Jinny had a child by Gipsy George, and her father built a cottage for them, on the site of the present tavern, which was then waste ground. Here they lived for a time, but when Gipsy George stole some sheep from Holloway, he was hanged at Tyburn. Jinny consoled herself for a while with a man called Darby, but after a few months of violent, drunken quarrelling, he disappeared, and no one ever heard what happened to him. Jinny's parents followed Gipsy George to the Tyburn gallows, when they were convicted of killing a young woman by black magic, and Jinny took up with a third lover, called Picher, who before long was found in her oven, burnt to a cinder.

Jinny was tried for murder but was acquitted, after a witness was produced and declared, no doubt through some sinister coercion, that Picher often took refuge in the oven, to escape the lash of Jinny's tongue, and could well have been burnt by accident – a tall story which must have taken a lot of swallowing.

By this time, Jinny's neighbours were mortally afraid of her and she became a recluse. She never appeared in daylight and how she lived no one knew: but at night time she was sometimes seen, haunting the lanes and hedgerows nearby, gathering herbs and berries.

During the Civil War, she gave shelter to a fugitive, who knocked at her door one night and begged for shelter. He had money and stopped with her for several years. From time to time they were heard to be quarrelling, but he stayed on, and although, when he died, there were whispers that she had poisoned him, nothing was ever proved against her, and he left her a considerable sum of money. Jinny lived on in the squalid little cottage, solitary and ill-favoured, and on the rare occasions when she was seen, she was always wearing an ugly old red cap and a dirty grey shawl, while her huge black cat was never far from her side. People were convinced that she was a witch, and for the most part were far too frightened to go near her, her only visitors being Moll Cut-purse, the highway-woman of Cromwell's time, who sometimes stayed with her for several weeks at a time, and a few brave souls who came to have their fortunes told or to be cured of some malady by one of her strange brews.

The night she died, people declared that they had seen the devil walk into the cottage, but no one ever saw him come out again. She died alone, sitting by the fire, her cat beside her. A broadsheet, describing her death, said: 'Mother Damnable was found the following morning, sitting before the fire-place, holding a crutch over it, with a tea-pot full of herbs, drugs and liquid.'

The cat was given some of this to drink, and 'its hair fell off in two hours, and the cat soon after died. . .the old woman's limbs were stiff and the undertaker had to break them before he could get her into her coffin'.

Another old woman moved into the tumble-down, thatched cottage after this, who was also called Mother Red Cap, but although the stories about her were often confused with those of the first terrible old woman, she was a far more cheerful and amiable character. In her girlhood, she had been a camp follower with the Duke of Marlborough's armies, and it was after the Treaty of Utrecht, in 1713, that she came here and turned the place into an inn. She brewed an especially potent and excellent ale, and Mother Red Cap's tavern soon became a favourite meeting place for soldiers who had known her when she was with the army.

PARLIAMENT HILL FIELDS

From Camden Town it is simplest to take the Northern Line tube again to Kentish Town, only one station away, for, from the walker's point of view, the best part of the journey begins from here. From the station, looking northwards, there are two roads, the left hand one being the Highgate Road, leading to Parliament Hill Fields (4) about twenty minutes' walk away. It is not far to walk, but a bus will also take you there.

No one knows for certain why this delightful stretch of heathland is called Parliament Hill. There is a tradition that it was here that Boadicea took poison and died, after her defeat at Battle Bridge, which has been located near King's Cross. There was a tumulus between Ken Wood and Parliament Hill, but when, at the end of the last century, it was excavated, no human remains were found, so the story is still unconfirmed.

Did the Guy Fawkes conspirators wait here, on the night of November 5th, 1605, hoping to watch the Parliament buildings blow up in a cloud of smoke and flames? This is another theory, although an unlikely one. Yet for many years afterwards the place was called Traitors' Fields.

During the Civil War the Parliamentary generals are said to have ordered cannon to be placed here, for the defence of London, and ever after they were known as Parliament Hill Fields: but yet another suggestion is that the name was not given to them until after the Middlesex elections were held here, during the seventeenth and eighteenth centuries.

THE GATE HOUSE

West Hill is a continuation of the Highgate Road and runs parallel and to the west of Highgate Hill. There is no bus to help you now, up this steep and winding but beautiful way, which was once the western boundary of the Baroness Burdett Coutts' estate of Holly Lodge, and which Coleridge called 'Widow Coutts' lane, where the nightingales sang'.

At the top of the hill, the Grove (6) branches off from West Hill and runs due north into Hampstead Lane. Here there are splendid 17th and 18th century houses, and at Number 3 Coleridge lived for many years with the Gillmans. South Grove (7) also branches off at this point, running north-eastwards, past Pond Square (5), and entering Highgate High Street. This is the summit of Highgate Hill and the centre of the old village. On

150

Highgate, the Grove.
British Tourist Authority

the corner of the *High Street* and *Hampstead Lane* stands the
Gate House tavern (**8**), where once there was a toll gate and an
arch which spanned the top of the road.

In early medieval times, beyond the summit of the hill
stretched the great Middlesex forest. The part of the forest to
the north of where the village of Highgate was to arise
belonged to St Albans Abbey, but William the Conqueror
appropriated it, as part of the royal forest reserved for the
King's hunts. He bestowed it at first on his half-brother Odo,
Bishop of Bayeux and Dean of Caen, but when Odo fell into
disfavour, the King gave it to the Bishopric of London: and as
it was in the parish of Hornsey, it was known as Hornsey Park.

It was enclosed, and succeeding Bishops built a hunting
lodge at the highest point, Lodge Hill, where today the
Highgate golf club lies. The lodge was a small square stone
castle, moated and approached by a drawbridge: and a private
road was built through the chase, its western gate being where
the Spaniards Inn was later to be established, and its eastern
gate a mile or so away at the top of Highgate Hill, about where
Highgate School (**9**) now stands. In this remote and lonely
spot, by the eastern gate, far away from any other dwelling, a

hermit established himself, his vocation being to act as gate-keeper to the Bishop.

By the fourteenth century, the Bishops of London were no longer keen huntsmen, as in Norman times, and the lodge became neglected and empty, but a succession of hermits still lived by the eastern gate, in the lonely little hermitage.

Trade throughout the country was increasing, and merchants and cattle drovers coming from the north to London still had to use the ruinous and muddy Roman Ermin Street, which approached the city by way of Crouch Hill and Muswell Hill. Eventually it became so bad that someone suggested asking the Bishop of London for permission to build a toll-road straight through his deserted wood, from Whetstone to the top of Highgate Hill. He agreed, and although there are no records of the building of the road, it is said that the hermit of the time, William Phelippe, did much of it single-handed, for there is a record, in 1364, of his reward by Edward III, who gave him permission to collect additional tolls from travellers, to reimburse him for his work and the expense of its maintenance, since:

'we highly commend the pious motive which for the advantage of our people. . .you unremittingly and continually exert in the emendation and support of that way in wood and sand, and other things of that nature necessary thereto at your own cost; and since you assert that your means are not sufficient for that purpose, we are willing upon due consideration to assent, and considering that those who from the performance of the said work obtain benefit and advantage to the same as is just. . .'

A toll gate was built, spanned by an arch, which at first was wide enough for only one loaded pack-horse at a time to pass through: and it was probably this gate which gave the village its name of Highgate. By this time there was a little chapel beside the hermitage, dedicated to St Michael, and here pilgrims would pause to worship, before continuing their way through the dark woods, by way of a narrow winding track, which is now Southwood Lane, to the shrine of Our Lady of Muswell Hill.

It was here that the friars of St John of Jerusalem had their farm and dairy, and they had built a chapel and convent for a small group of nuns, dedicated to our Lady of Muswell. Pilgrims came there to seek a cure for all manner of skin diseases, by drinking the miraculously curative waters of the sacred well, and amongst them was a certain King of Scotland, who was suffering from scrofula, and who, after drinking a draught from the holy well, was perfectly cured.

The Gate House, Highgate.
Marianne Taylor

DICK WHITTINGTON

It was during these medieval years of the fourteenth century that Dick Whittington, a poor orphan boy, came to London to seek his fortune, having heard that the streets were paved with gold and silver. He obtained work as a scullion in the house of a rich merchant, Sir Hugh Fitzwarren, but he had a miserable life, because of the cruelty of the cook.

He had allowed his only possession, his precious cat, to be taken aboard one of Sir Hugh's ships bound for Barbary, for the King of Barbary was in great distress, because his palace had been made uninhabitable by a plague of rats. Dick's cat caught every one of them and the King, in gratitude, had sent Dick a bag of wonderful treasure, but before he knew of this, the cook had made life so unbearable for him that he had run away.

He made his way northwards from the City, trudging through the fields of Islington and Holloway, until he reached the foot of Highgate Hill. Here he paused to rest by a stone cross for a while, and as he sat there he heard the bells of Bow Church, ringing across the meadows. 'Turn again, Whittington, Lord Mayor of London Town,' they seemed to be saying to him.

With renewed courage, he decided to return and try his fortune once more, so, marking the spot where he had first heard the bells, he set off again for London.

It is to be hoped that before he did this, he climbed to the top of the hill and followed the pilgrim way to Our Lady of Muswell Hill for a few yards, for the view of London from Southwood Lane is still superb and he could have heard Bow bells even more clearly and probably have seen the bell tower itself.

From that time, Dick's good luck never left him. He received the King of Barbary's fortune, which set him up for life, he married Sir Hugh's daughter, whom he had loved from the first moment he ever saw her, and duly became Mayor of London.

Romantic as it is, this story is only a legend, but it has become closely associated with the real Richard Whittington, the wealthy mercer who died in 1423. However, it was not told until the days of Queen Elizabeth, at a time when cats were in great demand abroad, particularly in South America, when it was first colonized by the Spaniards and Portuguese. Two cats, sent out to Cuyaba, in Brazil, where there was a plague of rats, are said to have been sold for a pound of gold. Their first kittens fetched thirty pieces of eight and the next generation twenty pieces, the price gradually falling as the cats multiplied.

A similar story to Dick's has been told of famous people in other countries and at different times, perhaps to explain the source of their wealth or other attributes. In a Persian manuscript of the tenth century, for example, is a story very like that of the pantomime Dick. Keis, the son of a poor widow, embarked for India, to seek his fortune, his sole possession being his cat. When he arrived, he found that the King's palace was so infested with rats and mice that the creatures were carrying the food from the royal banqueting table, and no one was able to catch them: but Keis' cat killed them all and they disappeared for ever, whereupon the King gave Keis a magnificent reward and he returned home to Persia a wealthy man and lived happily ever after.

Richard Whittington was the youngest son of Sir Richard Whittington of Gloucester. He was born in 1350, and became a mercer in the City of London. The one part of the legend which is true is that he married Alice, the daughter of Sir Ivo Fitzwaryn. He became a member of the Common Council, was elected an alderman and became a sheriff. When, in 1397, the Mayor died, the King appointed Richard to fill the office, and in the following year he was elected Mayor, the term Lord Mayor not being commonly used until Elizabethan times. He acquired great wealth and was 'mayor of the Staple' in both London and Calais, becoming Mayor of London again in 1406 and for a fourth term in 1419, only four years before he died.

The burning of coal was forbidden by Parliament during the fourteenth century, but by the time of Whittington's third mayoralty it was being used increasingly, despite the law, and coal from Newcastle to London became such an important part of the Thames commerce, that the law was amended. It has been said that Whittington made much of his wealth from this coal trade, and the fact that the colliers were called 'cats' would account for the association of his name with a cat, but this is probably just another legend, like the story of his gift to Henry V.

He had made frequent loans to both Henry IV and Henry V, and in 1421 he entertained Henry V and Queen Catherine at the Guildhall. The King at this time owed Richard £60,000, which he had advanced for the maintaining of the siege of Harfleur, which preceded the victory of Agincourt. The banquet was sumptuous and Whittington had even ordered precious woods, mixed with cinnamon and sweet smelling spices, to be burnt in the fires. The King, appreciating the lavishness of his hospitality, exclaimed: 'Surely, never had a prince such a subject. Even the fires are filled with perfume.'

'Surely, sire, never subject had such a King,' replied Whittington, and with that he picked up the King's bonds for £60,000, tore them in pieces and threw them into the flames.

Sir Richard lived in a mansion on College Hill, adjoining the ancient Church of St Michael, Paternoster Royal, where he was buried. The church was dedicated to the Archangel Michael, leader of the forces of good against evil, which was personified by Lucifer, the fallen angel of light. It was close to Paternoster Lane, where all the rosaries were made, and the 'Royal' is a corruption of La Réole, the town near Bordeaux from which the merchants of the Vintry, close by in Upper Thames Street, imported their wine.

Sir Richard's wife, Alice, died before him and they had no children, so he left his fortune to maintain the large number of charities he had begun during his lifetime, including the College of Priests he founded at Paternoster Royal and the adjoining hospital and almshouses. The College was dissolved at the Reformation, but the hospital and almshouses survived and were moved to Highgate.

His tomb in the old Church, before the rebuilding after the Great Fire, was a magnificent affair of carved marble, and there is a story that, during the reign of Edward VI, an incumbent of the church, believing it to be full of gold and rich jewels, broke it open. He found nothing, and in a rage of disappointment, he smashed up the entire tomb. It was said that Sir Richard's body was later moved, but no one knows where. In 1949, after the church had been severely damaged by flying bombs, another search was made for it, but, strangely enough, all that turned up was the body of a mummified cat.

The church has been restored and re-dedicated: and part of it is now the headquarters of the Mission to Seamen.

SWEARING ON THE HORNS

With the Reformation, the ancient Hermitage at the top of Highgate Hill was abandoned, but the archway remained, by now a solid brick gateway, with rooms above it. At the western end, the first Gate House tavern was soon established, for the ever increasing number of travellers, in particular the cattle drovers, on their way to Smithfield. Here the first ceremony of 'Swearing on the Horns' was established, which in time was to be inflicted by the landlords of all the Highgate taverns on everyone passing through the village for the first time.

It was a light-hearted affair. The traveller was first invited to submit to the ceremony, and having agreed, a pair of stag's horns, fixed to a long pole, was produced by the clerk of the ceremony, while the landlord donned a black cloak, mask and wig. The assembled company bared their heads and the landlord recited the oath, a nonsensical affair, which included such rejoinders as: 'You must acknowledge me to be your adopted father, I must acknowledge you to be my adopted son. If you do not call me father, you forfeit a bottle of wine; if I do not call you son I forfeit the same. And now, my good sir, if you are travelling through the village of Highgate, and you have no money in your pocket, go call for a bottle of wine at any house you may think proper to enter, and book it to your father's score . . .You must not kiss the maid while you can kiss the mistress, unless you like the maid the best; but sooner than miss a good chance you may kiss them both. . .'

And after a good deal more in the same vein, the traveller was given the freedom of Highgate. At the Gate House, the drovers would watch their victim carefully, and if he submitted cheerfully to the last command, which was 'So now, my son, God bless you! Kiss the horns – or a pretty girl if you see one here, which you like best, and so be free to Highgate', he was regarded as a suitable companion for the rest of the evening and welcomed to join the bibulous company of the regulars.

The ceremony went on all through the seventeenth and eighteenth centuries and even into the days of the Regency, by which time there were nineteen inns in Highgate, all of them equipped with horns for the ceremony, but the arch by the Gate House, which had remained long after carts and carriages had become too large to go under it, and had to be diverted through the inn yard, was demolished in 1769.

THE GHOST OF POND SQUARE

One snowy winter's day in 1626, Sir Francis Bacon was driving with Dr Winterborn, the King's Scottish physician, towards Highgate, when it suddenly occurred to him that snow might preserve the human body in the same way as salt. He and the doctor decided then and there to experiment. They stopped the coach at the bottom of Highgate Hill, bought a hen from a cottager, who killed and drew it for them, and then proceeded to stuff it with snow. It was such a cold day, however, that Sir Francis was taken suddenly ill with a severe chill, and the doctor decided he must be put to bed somewhere in Highgate, before returning to his lodgings in Gray's Inn. They chose the Earl of Arundel's house in South Grove (**7**), which was where the seventeenth-century Old Hall now stands. They were welcomed, but unfortunately the bed offered to Sir Francis was damp and he never recovered, dying there a few days later.

The tail piece to this story is that the hen has haunted Pond Square (**5**) ever since, its wings flapping dismally, in protest at having been made the victim of the first experiment in refrigeration.

Pond Square, Highgate Village.
British Tourist Authority

LAUDERDALE HOUSE AND ARABELLA STUART

*Walk down the High Street and Highgate Hill, for they are full of interest and it is barely a mile to the nearest underground station. On your right is Waterlow Park (**10**),* and Sir William Waterlow's house is still there, where once stood an Elizabethan mansion, Lauderdale House, one of the many reputed homes of Nell Gwyn, lent to her for a time by the Earl of Lauderdale. It was from an upstairs window of Lauderdale House that she is said to have held out her baby to Charles II, standing below in the garden, and called: 'If you don't do something for your son, here he goes!', whereupon the King cried: 'Stop Nelly. Save the Earl of Burford!' And the Earl of Burford grew up to become the Duke of St Albans.

At the beginning of the seventeenth century, Lauderdale House was owned by Alderman Sir William Bond, and it was here that poor Arabella Stuart was lodged, on her way to captivity in Durham, after King James had ordered her arrest for secretly marrying William Seymour, against his wishes: for together they formed a grave threat to the succession to the throne.

Seymour was consigned to the Tower, but somehow, no one knows how, he and Arabella contrived a plan of escape. Dressed in men's clothes, Arabella managed to get away from Lauderdale House and reached the meeting place at Leigh, in the Thames estuary, where they were to embark for France: and Seymour, heavily disguised, made his successful escape from the Tower.

The plan went wrong when Arabella's attendants became too nervous to wait for his arrival and insisted on her embarking on the French barque waiting for them. Seymour arrived shortly afterwards, hiring a fishing boat and hoping to catch up with them.

In the meantime, their escape was discovered and the King at once ordered a pinnace to give chase. They caught Arabella and brought her back to the Tower, but Seymour in his fishing boat, not knowing what had happened to his beloved Arabella, reached the French coast safely. Arabella remained in the Tower, never allowed to know what had happened to her husband or receive any letter from him, and four years later she died there, many said of a broken heart.

It was after Bond's death that the house came into the possession of the Earl of Lauderdale, and during the Civil War when, after the battle of Worcester, he was sent to the Tower, John Ireton, the brother of Cromwell's son-in-law Henry Ireton, lived there, while in the cottage just above it Andrew Marvell lived, while he was working for Milton and was a member of the Commonwealth Parliament. The cottage has now been demolished, but a plaque in the wall of the park marks the site.

Just opposite on the east side of the hill, is the magnificent Cromwell House, a Jacobean mansion which tradition says Cromwell built for Henry Ireton, but this seems to be a fallacy, the only connexion being Thomas Ireton's occupation of Lauderdale House, which was short, for at the Restoration he hurriedly departed and Lauderdale returned.

Cromwell House was in the possession of the Sprigwell family from 1605 until several years after the Restoration and was then sold to another wealthy family, the Hills.

Lauderdale House.
Marianne Taylor

160

DICK WHITTINGTON AGAIN

At the foot of the hill, below St Joseph's Retreat, is the Whittington Stone, marking the spot where Dick is said to have rested, when he ran away from the Fitzwarrens' cook. It has been replaced several times. The original stone was thought to have been part of a wayside cross set up in front of the Lazar House and Chapel of St Anthony, which stood here until the last years of the Commonwealth, but it could well have been a fragment of an old mounting block. The inscription on the present stone does not perpetuate the legend, but a sleepy looking, recumbent cat surmounts it, with a rather wary expression, as though well aware that he had no real right to be there, but has every intention of remaining.

On both sides of the road there is ample evidence of Whittington's beneficence, the large Whittington hospital (**12**).

The Archway station, on the Northern Line, is ahead of you, to take you back to Tottenham Court Road.

FROM HIGHGATE HILL TO HAMPSTEAD

Murder by Black Magic

*Kenwood House, The Spaniards and
Jack Straw's Castle*

The Highwaymen of Hampstead Heath

Lord Chatham at Wildwood House

Hampstead Spa

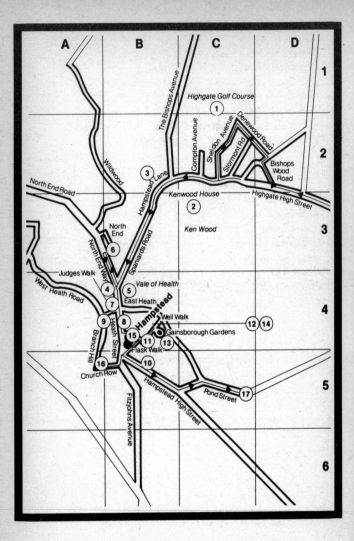

H

1 Highgate Golf Course
2 Kenwood House and Ken Wood
3 The Spaniards
4 Jack Straw's Castle
5 Vale of Health
6 North End and Wildwood – Old Bull and Bush
7 Whitestone Pond
8 Heath Street
9 Judge's Walk
10 Hampstead High Street
11 Flask Walk
12 Well Walk
13 Gainsborough Gardens
14 Burgh House
15 New End
16 Church Row
17 Pond Street

H

BUSES
Highgate Village: 143, 210, 271.
Hampstead Road/Spaniards Road: 210.
Heath Street: 268.
Hampstead High Street: 268.
Pond Street: 187.

This is only a rough guide to the buses and you may need to consult the London Transport Bus Map.

UNDERGROUNDS
Hampstead

MURDER BY BLACK MAGIC

From the Gate House at the top of Highgate High Street turn along Hampstead Lane. On your right, where once was the Bishop of London's hunting ground, there are now sports grounds and pleasant avenues. Bishopswood Road on your right is the clue to the history of the ground, and this will bring you to the Highgate golf club (**1**), *via Denewood Road, the site of a strange scene of* necromancy, which took place not twenty years after the death of Richard Whittington.

In 1440, Eleanor, Duchess of Gloucester, during the quarrels and jealousies which were to culminate in the vicious Wars of the Roses, devised a plot to destroy the young King Henry VI by black magic. She engaged Roger Bolingbroke, the astrologer, and Margery Jourdain, the witch, to help her, while Thomas Southwell, a canon of St Stephen's, Westminster, was recruited to say masses for the soul of the departed King, after their work was completed. Their plan was to make a wax model of the King and then destroy it, when, by the age-old principle of sympathetic magic, strengthened by suitable spirits of evil invoked by Bolingbroke, the King himself would die, leaving no evidence of either violence or poisoning: and the place they chose for their midnight ceremony, deep in the dark woods, was the lonely Bishop's hunting lodge, deserted now for a hundred years, its moat dry and choked with scrub and trees, its towers haunted by owls and bats. Margery Jourdain was to make the little model of the King and Bolingbroke to commit the act of destruction.

At the last minute, their courage forsook them. The Duchess fled to the sanctuary of Westminster, but suspicions had already been aroused. Bolingbroke was arrested and confessed, though putting the blame fully on the Duchess. All four were tried and convicted of 'endeavouring to consume the king's person by necromantic art'. Southwell, having said masses over the instruments which were to be used for that purpose, was committed to the Tower, where he died. Bolingbroke was hanged, drawn and quartered at Tyburn. Margery Jourdain was burnt at Smithfield, and the Duchess was condemned to do penance through the streets of London. On the first day she was brought from Westminster to the Temple, where she landed. Then, with a tall wax taper in her hand, she had to walk bareheaded and barefoot to St Paul's, where, at the high altar, she offered prayers for her forgiveness. The next day she did penance at Christchurch, Aldgate, and on the third day at St Michael's, Cornhill, and on each day she was followed in solemn procession by the mayor, the sheriffs and members of the corporation. Then she was banished to the Isle of Man and locked up in Peel Castle, which they say is haunted, to this day, by her ghost.

KENWOOD HOUSE, THE SPANIARDS AND JACK STRAW'S CASTLE

On the left side of Hampstead Lane stretch the grounds of Kenwood House (2) and here is the main entrance. It was once known as Caen Wood, which confirms the belief that this part of Highgate once belonged to Odo, Dean of Caen.

The house was rebuilt for the first Earl of Mansfield by Robert Adam, and the wonderful collection of pictures, on view to the public today, is part of the Iveagh bequest. The lovely garden, with its woods and magnificent beech trees, was much of it designed by Lord Mansfield himself, although in later years, during the time of the second Earl, Humphrey Repton took a hand.

The finest room in the house is the library, with its domed ceiling painted by Zucchi. The ceiling of the entrance hall also has a painted panel, and for a long time it was said to have been the work of Angelica Kauffmann, the story being that here, in the idyllic setting of Kenwood House, the two first met and fell in love, but it must have been somewhere else – perhaps Luton Hoo – for although they did fall in love and marry, after Angelica's first disastrous marriage to the bigamist and bogus Count Frederick de Horn, the ceiling of Kenwood House hall was painted by Biagio Rebecca.

Ken Wood is on the border of Highgate and Hampstead, and after a short walk down the Hampstead Lane, which runs along the crest of the Heath, the way turns southwards to become the

A view of Kenwood House, from an engraving by John Boydell, 1781.

Spaniards Road, and here, on the corner, is the Spaniards Inn (**3**), standing on the site of the gatekeeper's lodge, built at the western end of the road through the Bishop's Wood.

Why the inn is called The Spaniards no one knows for certain, but the generally accepted story is that it was established by a Spanish family who had come to England as servants of the Spanish Ambassador some time in the late sixteenth century.

During the Gordon riots, Lord Mansfield's house in Bloomsbury Square was burned to the ground by the rioting mob and Lord and Lady Mansfield escaped only just in time, by the back door. The rioters then rampaged northwards, determined to burn down his country mansion too.

As they stormed up the hill from Hampstead, the landlord of The Spaniards, Giles Thomas, prepared for them. It was a blazing hot day and the men had come a long way. He welcomed them, assumed a sympathy for their cause and offered them free beer and a rest, before they went on to do battle with the servants of Kenwood House. Gratefully they accepted the offer, and Thomas produced every barrel of beer in the inn, to slake their thirsts. Then he sent secretly to the steward of Kenwood House for more supplies, and at the same time to the barracks for a detachment of horse-guards.

The steward soon had every barrel of beer in Kenwood House up from the cellars, and they were emptied into tubs along the roadside. The rioters had the time of their lives and when at last the guards arrived, they were all so drunk that they were easily persuaded to return to London, noisily, no doubt, but harmlessly, and Kenwood House was saved.

In the coming years, a tea-garden was attached to The Spaniards, and it became a favourite spot for summer visitors from London, including, of course, Dickens' Mrs Bardell and her friends, who were enjoying their tea and bread and butter, when Mr Jackson arrived with old Isaac, and persuading her to return to London on urgent legal business, delivered her to the Fleet prison, for not paying her lawyer's bill. And to add to the wicked old woman's alarm and mortification, she came face to face with Mr Pickwick, whom she had so grievously wronged.

The Spaniards Road runs southwards across the Heath for about half a mile, with the Vale of Health (5) on the eastern side, and just before joining Heath Street stands Jack Straw's Castle (4), not long rebuilt after its severe bomb damage of World War Two. Jack Straw was a generic name for a farm labourer, as Jack Tar is for a sailor, and this may have been the rallying point for the labourers of Hampstead and the surrounding villagers, on their way to join Wat Tyler's march on London, during the Peasants' Revolt of 1381.

The Vale of Health, Hampstead.
Marianne Taylor

THE HIGHWAYMEN OF HAMPSTEAD HEATH

During the seventeenth and eighteenth centuries, highwaymen were a menace on this lonely stretch of the Heath. Claude Duval helped to create the myth of the 'Gentleman' highwayman. He was a young Frenchman, who had come over to England at the Restoration, in the service of the Duke of Richmond, but he soon left him, to take to the roads. At first he worked between Islington and Highgate, along the Holloway Road, but then turned his attention to Hampstead and the Heath. And it was here that Macaulay says he stopped a lady's coach, in which 'there was a booty of £400. He took only £100 and suffered the fair owner to ransom the rest by dancing a coranto with him on the heath'.

He seems gradually to have worked westwards, for Platts Lane, in West Hampstead, running into the Finchley Road, was once called Duval's Lane, and was said to be so infested with highwaymen, that few people would venture along it, even in daylight. Yet Duval did not have a very long run, for in 1669, when he was still only twenty-six years old, he was caught, in Mother Maberley's tavern, the Hole-in-the-Wall, in Chandos Street, Covent Garden, where the Marquis of Granby now stands. After being hanged at Tyburn, his body was brought back to lie in state at the Tangier tavern in St Giles, and then, at dead of night, he was given a splendid funeral at St Paul's, Covent Garden, attended by a crowd of weeping women, who had fallen in love with his good looks and insidious charm. He is said to have been buried in the central aisle of the church, and his epitaph read:

'Here lies Duval, Reader, if male thou art
Look to thy purse, if female, to thy heart'

but today no trace of it can be found.

The records list dozens of attacks on the Heath by highwaymen, many of them ending in murder, and those who were caught were hanged on the two gibbet elms growing near Jack Straw's Castle, the last of which blew down in a storm in 1907.

The body of Francis Jackson, the highwayman who attacked and murdered Henry Miller at Hampstead, was strung up on the gibbet elms from 1673 until 1691, by which time his skeleton had completely disintegrated, but this seemed in no way to deter his brothers in crime, for during the following years their numbers actually increased.

Sixteen-String Jack worked in Hampstead and in 1718 Dick Turpin arrived in London, from his home in Saffron Walden, to begin his apprenticeship to a Whitechapel butcher.

Dick was gay and companionable and soon made friends who were far better off than himself. He gambled and dressed well, to keep up with them, and was very soon in debt: and to pay his debts, he became a successful footpad. At the end of his apprenticeship, he returned home, married and set up a butcher's business in Thaxted, but he was lazy and conceited, and when it failed he moved to Sewardstone and tried again. As the bills mounted, he took to cattle and sheep stealing, and when suspicion fell on him, he deserted his wife and fled, taking to the life of a fugitive criminal. He joined the notorious Gregory gang of housebreakers, but before long they were all caught and hanged, except Dick, who now became a highwayman. One day, while lying in wait on a lonely road, he saw a likely victim approaching and rode out to meet him, with the all too familiar words: 'Stand and deliver!' The man burst out laughing, for he was Robert King, the Gentleman Highwayman, and recognized Dick. They became firm friends and for some time worked together, robbing travellers in Epping forest, on Finchley Common and on the heaths of Hounslow and Hampstead.

King was as notorious a rogue as Dick and affected an air of gallantry, which Dick copied, continuing the false air of glamour which had surrounded Duval. Even Sir John Fielding wrote that 'highwaymen are civil as compared with other countries; do not often use you with ill-manners' and have been 'frequently known to return papers and curiosities with much politeness; and never commit murder, unless they are hotly pursued and find it difficult to escape'.

This was cold comfort to their victims and public resentment against them grew stronger every year. Soon Dick and King found it difficult to persuade innkeepers to give them a bed for the night, or even a meal, despite a substantial bribe, but there is a story that the landlord of The Spaniards – a very different character from Giles Thomas apparently – gave him spare keys to the toll-gate and to a secret door, which led from the back of the inn to the stables, so that, in an emergency, he could make a quick escape.

Eventually Dick and King had to resort to a secret cave in the depths of Epping forest, reversing their horses' shoes, to avoid being trailed there. King was at last caught, being mortally wounded in the last fight, but Dick managed to escape back to the forest, killing one of the foresters on the way. With a price on his head as a murderer, he rode up to Lincoln, changing his name to John Palmer, and establishing himself for a time as a cattle and horse dealer. Yet he was incapable of living honestly, and was soon stealing the animals before he sold them. Once more he had to make a quick departure and headed for York, where he was eventually recognized, tried, convicted and hung. The story of his dramatic ride from London to York is pure fantasy, the legend having been told of some other villain, three hundred years earlier: but conceited and a dandy to the last, he did buy himself a new coat and shoes for his execution, and black hat-bands and gloves for the five mourners whom he had hired to follow him to the gallows.

LORD CHATHAM AT WILDWOOD HOUSE

Before turning south from Jack Straw's Castle into Heath Street, walk back a little way up North End Way, until you come to the Old Bull and Bush (**6**). Before this became a pub, it was a farmhouse, which William Hogarth bought for his country home. Behind it runs Sandy Lane, running back to The Spaniards, which John Turner built about 1750, and along it houses were soon built, set in spacious grounds. The largest of them was North End Place, which until its demolition in 1952 was known under several names, Wildwood House, Wildwoods and Pitt House, standing in a short lane running northwards from Sandy Road.

It was here that, for nearly a year, William Pitt lived in a strange retirement, shortly after he was raised to the peerage and became Lord Chatham. People were told that he was suffering from gout, but it seems to have been a form of melancholia which was near to madness. Lord Grenville's secretary reported that 'he sits all day leaning on his hands, which he supports on the table; does not permit any person to remain in the room; knocks when he wants anything; and, having made his wants known, gives a signal without speaking to the person who answered his call, to retire'.

Most of the time he spent in a small room, little more than a closet, on the third floor of the mansion. There was an opening in the wall, about eighteen inches square, giving on to the staircase, with a door on either side of the wall: and the inner door was kept padlocked. When meals or messages were taken to him, the messenger knocked on the outer door and placed them in the recess, but not until he had heard this outer door shut again would the Prime Minister unlock his side, take them and lock himself in again.

Occasionally he was taken for a drive about the loneliest part of the Heath, in a carriage with drawn blinds, but no one in Hampstead knew who he was.

In a short period of sanity, he offered his resignation to King George III, but the King would not accept it and by the autumn of 1768 he began to recover, although he now formally resigned office. For the next ten years he lived on, occasionally appearing in the House of Lords and sometimes able to speak with a spark of his earlier grandeur and eloquence, especially when trying to avert the American War of Independence, but it was in the House that he finally collapsed, dying a few weeks later.

For many years the room in the house where he had suffered his strange illness was preserved, and to add to the melancholy story, the garden was said to have been haunted by the ghost of a maidservant, who during these years, was murdered by the butler, in the summer house.

When the house was demolished, two modern houses were built on the site, but there is a plaque on the garden wall recording Lord Chatham's stay there, and no one has seen the ghost of the unfortunate maidservant for a long time now.

A Hampstead Lane.
Marianne Taylor

HAMPSTEAD SPA

It is time to return to Heath Street (8) and reach the heart of Hampstead. On your right, just below Jack Straw's Castle (4) and the Whitestone Pond (7), you will see Judge's Walk (9), which is said to have been the spot where, during the Great Plague, the judges held their courts under the trees: and it was once known as King's Bench Avenue.

Until the end of the seventeenth century, Hampstead was still a rural village, prospering on dairy farming, although already there was an unusual number of mansions close by, for wealthy Londoners had begun to appreciate the clean, fresh air of these northern heights, after the dirt and smoke of the City: but its sudden conversion into a gay and busy little town was because of the development of its mineral springs, which made it, for a few years, a fashionable spa.

There are many springs round the edge of the Heath, occurring where the porous and permeable sand of the top soil joins the relatively impermeable clay beneath it, and some of these springs are chalybeate – impregnated with iron – which was believed to have curative properties for all manner of ills.

The legend of their magical healing powers was first told during the reign of King Ethelred, when he granted the manor of Hampstead to the church at Westminster. At that time a monk brought from Tours to the little colony of monks from Westminster living at Hampstead, a precious phial containing four tears of the Virgin Mary. One day, while praying in the field, he dropped the phial and the tears were lost, sinking into the ground. He was sadly troubled, but that night he had a consoling dream, telling him that if he returned to the spot where he had lost the tears he would find a healing spring.

He found the spring, which was said to have been near Well Walk (**12**), where the other springs were later to be developed. The tradition must have been kept alive through the centuries, but the first indication of anyone having benefited from the waters came with the discovery of a halfpenny token, made during the reign of Charles II, bearing on one side the inscription 'Dorothy Rippon at the Well in Hamsted' and on the other the representation of a well and bucket.

Then, in 1689, by which time the Manor of Hampstead had come back, after the Restoration, into the possession of the Camdens, the family bequeathed 'six acres of waste land lying and being about certain medicinal waters called the Wells, for the sole use, benefit and advantage of the poor of the parish of Hampstead successively for ever'.

At first, the trustees of this bequest arranged for the waters to be collected from the springs and taken to the Flask tavern – standing on the site of the present Flask in *Flask Walk* (**11**), *which is the first turning on the left, after entering the High Street* (**10**) *from Heath Street.* Here it was bottled and taken by carriers to a number of London taverns, where it was sold for 3d a bottle. Sales were so encouraging that the Trustees then decided on more ambitious plans, offering to lease the six acres to a speculator prepared to develop them into a Spa which would compare with Bath and Tunbridge Wells.

By June of 1701, John Duffield had leased the land and one of the springs, the main spring, from which the flask water was obtained, being still in the hands of the Trustees, as a separate venture.

Duffield built a large Assembly Room, more usually known as the Great Room, on the site of what is now *Gainsborough Gardens* (**13**), *on the east side of Well Walk:* and in the tradition of the fashionable Spas of these years, equipped it with a concert room, a ballroom, and smaller rooms for cards, while for the genuine invalids was the pump room, with a large basin, into which flowed the healing waters of the chalybeate spring.

Flask Walk, Hampstead.
Marianne Taylor

Although he was very short of money and soon had to borrow, he spared no expense, and the surrounding grounds were laid out with flower beds and lawns, an ornamental lake and a bowling green.

Dr Gibbons, already a resident of Hampstead, promoted the Spa, declaring that the waters 'were fully as efficacious in all cases where ferruginous waters are advised as any chalybeate waters in England', and he moved into his handsome new Burgh House (14), which still stands, on the west side of Well Walk.

For the first few years of the eighteenth century the Spa was a great success. The concerts and balls were advertised in the London papers, with a note that for those returning to London the same night, the management provided a special armed guard, with torches and links, to accompany them on the four-mile journey, as a safeguard against thieves and highwaymen. The rich and fashionable flocked to Hampstead, enjoying the fresh air, the beauty of the Heath and the gaiety of the entertainments. Houses to accommodate visitors who stayed for the cure were built, including the delightful cottages of Squire's Mount. Before long some had decided to live permanently in Hampstead, and it was during these years that so many of the attractive Queen Anne and Georgian houses were built, in Pond Street (17) and Heath Street, and on the steep hills running up to the Heath. This, with New End (15), was the only ground available, for the owners of the flatter, highly valuable agricultural land were unwilling to part with it.

The development of Hampstead and an account of the famous men and women, writers, poets and artists who, from this time, came to live here, belong to history, but the healing properties of the chalybeate waters are only legendary, for although Dr Gibbons remained faithful to them all his life, there were several doubters, even from the outset, including Sir Samuel Garth, the eminent poet-physician, who was appointed Physician-in-Ordinary to George I. Nevertheless, many sick people did benefit from a stay in Hampstead, because of the invigorating fresh air.

In 1705, Duffield announced that he had provided a cold bath in connection with 'one of the best springs on the Heath, lying between the Old Green and New Green, adjoyning the Spaw-waters', with 'all conveniences for hot and cold bathing', but we hear very little more of it, except that it was destroyed by the great frost of 1708, and four years later, after it had been repaired, it was reported to be 'in better order than usual'.

Hampstead gained a further distinction when the aristocratic Kit-Kat Club, dedicated to establishing the Hanoverian succession, decided to hold their summer meetings at the Upper Flask tavern, which was just at the top of Heath Street, where Queen Mary's Maternity Home now stands. Its members included the most distinguished Whigs of the day, the Duke of Marlborough, five other Dukes, Lord Halifax, Sir Robert Walpole, Congreve, Sir Samuel Garth, Vanburgh, Godfrey Kneller, Addison and Steele, and they sat for hours under the famous mulberry tree in the Upper Flask garden, talking, drinking, arguing and debating. After 1714, however, when George I succeeded to the throne, the Club had served its purpose, and a few years later it was disbanded.

It was to the Upper Flask that Samuel Richardson's Clarissa Harlowe fled, after she had been abducted by Lovelace and taken to a disreputable sponging house in Kentish Town.

She went into the Upper Flask and asked for a dish of tea and a room to herself for half an hour. Then, finding herself pursued by Lovelace's accomplices, she ran off towards Hendon, passing by the sign of the 'Castle' on the Heath.

But this was in the middle of the eighteenth century, by which time Duffield's Spa had had its day, for its life was very short.

The gaming tables had proved the greatest attraction, and soon betting shops opened, followed by the card sharpers, who could easily reach Hampstead from London. The character of the concerts changed, and by 1706 they were including fairground tumblers and ladder-dancers. By 1709, John Mackey was writing that Hampstead, by 'its nearness to London brought so many loose women in vampt-up clothes to catch the City apprentices, that modest company are ashamed to appear here . . .it seems to be overstok'd with Jews and sharpers'.

The days of high fashion were over and when the Hampstead

Fair was established, in 1712, 'to be kept upon the Lower Flask Tavern and holds for four days', the end was very near.

Duffield struggled on, but it was the betting shops which prospered now, and Old Mother Huff, who behind the cover of a respectable tea-garden on the Spaniard's Road, ran a house of assignation, told fortunes and was generally regarded as practising witchcraft, while Jenny Diver, the pick-pocket, had a good run at Hampstead, until she was finally caught and hanged at Tyburn.

The constables began to visit. The gaming tables and betting shops were declared illegal and quickly disappeared. Duffield was bankrupt, the original trustees of the Wells Charity were nearly all dead, and the Gainsborough family, who had descended from the Camdens, no longer owned the Manor.

Dr Gibbons died in 1725, still proclaiming the virtues of the chalybeate waters, and it was in this year that the Assembly Room was turned into an episcopal chapel. Houses were built where the betting shops had once stood. Mother Huff retired to The Hoop and Bunch of Grapes at North End, and Hampstead settled down for a spell, into well-bred quietness and solitude.

In 1734, however, the waters found a new champion in Dr John Soames of Hampstead, who had been a friend of Dr Gibbon. He published a pamphlet, in which he regretted that the waters had fallen into neglect, through 'the knavery of some and the folly of others', praised their healing powers in 'cutaneous and nervous disorders, as well as those of debility' and extolled the beauties of Hampstead and its 'pure and balmy Air'.

He assured his readers that the chalybeate water, 'though as strong if not stronger, than that of Tunbridge Wells of the iron mineral, is not at all unpleasant: that if well corked and sealed down, and kept in a cellar for one or two years, when you have drawn the cork it will be most ready to fly, and when poured into a glass, will sparkle and knit up like a glass of champagne or Herefordshire cider!'

At the same time, he condemned the drinking of tea, which he alleged was reducing the stature of the nation, and if continued, would cause 'the next generation to be more like pygmies than men and women', but approved of tobacco. 'They that take tobacco may do it here with all the safety in the World; but let them have a regard not to offend the company, especially the ladies, who cannot well relish that smoke with their waters'.

The best time to take the waters, he said, was between June and Michaelmas, at an hour after sunrise, which was an echo of Dr Gibbons' regimen. He allowed sage tea, with a little orange peel, for breakfast, or chocolate, milk, porridge or mutton broth, with bread and butter: and an hour after taking the waters, the patient might take coffee – though on no account tea – after which he recommended a ride of four or five miles, 'because, by the Motion of the Horse, the Stomach and Viscera are thereby borne up and contracted, by which means the Waters will be better digested'.

This pamphlet received an enthusiastic reception and within a few months building began on a new Long Room, this time on the west side of Well Walk, near Burgh House, and where today the Wells Council flats stand. Though we hear little

Early eighteenth-century town houses in Church Row.
British Tourist Authority

enough of the curative properties of the waters, this second venture was more successful, and conducted on infinitely more decorous lines than the first Spa, even though Fanny Burney's Evelina had such a miserable evening, when Mr Smith invited her and her grandmother, Madame Duval, to a ball there. The book was published in 1778, when the Long Room had become a favourite meeting place for the people of Hampstead, but Evelina disliked Mr Smith and thought that he and her grandmother were both vulgarly overdressed, and the old lady was wearing too much rouge.

The Long Room was still popular ten years later, for in 1788 Anna Barbauld was writing to Samuel Rogers that 'we are to have an Assembly in the Long Room on Monday next, the 2nd, which they say will be a pretty good one. I take the liberty to ask you whether it will be agreeable to you to be of our party. . .'

But the Long Room had not much longer to run. Its fortunes gradually flagged and at last it closed and the contents, including wine and plate, were auctioned, the sale being advertised in 1794, in the *Morning Chronicle*, as the property of Mr Jonas Fox, Vintner, a Bankrupt.

The Room became a private house, known after its first occupier as Weatherall House. Later it was the home of John Masefield, and after his death it was pulled down to make way for the present Council flats.

And the chalybeate waters? In 1902 Dr Littlejohn, then the medical officer of health for Hampstead, reported that, after a careful examination, it must be said that the chalybeate water of the Well Walk fountain, and a further sample obtained by sinking a shaft, 'cannot be used for drinking purposes without danger to health'.

By this time, of course, the waters were no doubt heavily polluted, but nevertheless, it seems that Sir Samuel Garth was right and they had never had any medicinal value. So Hampstead was built on a legend, yet so much remains that is beautiful, including Church Row (**16**), one of the finest surviving terraces of early eighteenth-century town houses in the whole country, that it was all well worth while.

FROM PICCADILLY CIRCUS TO KENSINGTON

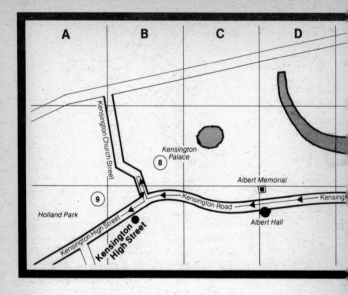

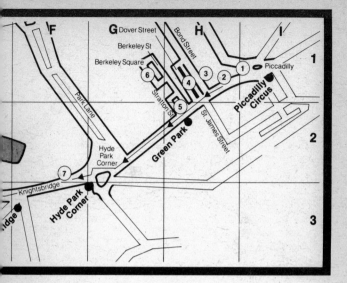

I

I

BUSES
Piccadilly: 9, 14, 19, 22, 38.
Berkeley Square/Piccadilly: 25.
Knightsbridge: 9, 14, 19, 22, 30, 52, 73, 74, 137.
Kensington Road: 9, 52, 73.
Kensington High Street: 9, 27, 28, 31, 33, 49, 73.

This is only a rough guide and you may need to consult the London Transport Bus Map.

UNDERGROUNDS
Piccadilly
Green Park
Hyde Park Corner
Knightsbridge
Kensington High Street

THE GHOSTS OF BERKELEY SQUARE

From Piccadilly Circus it is only a quarter of an hour's stroll down Piccadilly to Berkeley Square (**6**), and on the way you will pass many relics of Mayfair's former grandeur. Before the Restoration, this land was countryside, a place of fields and farmlands, watered by the little Tyburn stream, and the only buildings were one or two scattered farmhouses and a solitary windmill.

The building began when Charles II granted his Chancellor, Lord Clarendon, thirty acres of these fields and he began planning his magnificent palace, Clarendon House. After that, the building of Mayfair proceeded steadily, and the first building of Stuart times you will pass is Albany (**1**), hidden away in its quiet courtyard. This was originally Lord Sunderland's house, but it passed eventually into the possession of Lord Melbourne, who employed William Chambers to alter and enlarge it, and Cipriani to paint the ceiling of the beautiful ballroom. In 1791 Lord Melbourne exchanged it with the Duke of York, for the Duke's house in Whitehall, but the Duke did not live there long, and in 1803 Melbourne House was converted into the present chambers, called Albany, after the Duke's second title.

The next important survival in Piccadilly is Burlington House (**2**), which was built for the first Lord Burlington, on land bought from Clarendon's thirty acres, and it was here that poor Pepys, on an evening visit, stood too near one of the candles and set his wig on fire.

Lord George Cavendish, who inherited the house, employed Samuel Ware to make many alterations to the old mansion, and he also commissioned him to build the Burlington Arcade adjoining it. Lord George maintained the tradition of hospitality which had always been associated with Burlington House, but after his death it fell empty, and in 1834 the family sold it to the government: and thus it became the home of the Royal Academy, as well as of numerous learned societies. New buildings arose on the beautiful garden at the back, and in 1868 Colin Campbell's colonnades and front wall came down and the present frontage was built to the courtyard.

Passing the Burlington Arcade (**3**) *and crossing Old Bond*

Street, we come to the site of Clarendon House (4), where Albemarle Street and Dover Street now run. Clarendon House had a tragically short life. The architect, Roger Pratt, planned a house far exceeding in splendour and cost anything that Clarendon had first conceived. Building began in 1664 and was not completed until 1667, by which time he had fallen into disfavour with the King and the country. He was blamed for all the troubles of those years, the Dutch war, the sale of Dunkirk, the plague, the Great Fire, and even the barrennesss of the Queen. His wife had died and he was crippled with gout – but he had fallen in love with his magnificent new palace, and moved in, to live in solitary state. Only a few weeks later, King Charles asked him to return his seals of office. John Evelyn visited him that evening and said that he found him in his wheel-chair, very sad, but superintending the setting up of the gates at the back of the house, on to the fields. By the next morning, he had fled secretly to France, never to return, for he had been warned that he was to be impeached for high treason.

Clarendon House was let for a time and then bought by the young Duke of Albemarle, who soon ran through all his money, as we have seen, and sold it to a building syndicate: and less than twenty years after the first stone of the mansion had been laid, it was completely demolished.

Clarendon had also sold part of his thirty acres, to the west of Clarendon House, to Lord Berkeley of Stratton, who built here Berkeley House: but after his death, in 1684, Lady Berkeley sold some of the land at the back of the house to another building syndicate, and it was here that Berkeley Square (6) was to be built, while the house itself was bought by the Devonshires, and became the first Devonshire House (5).

By this time the streets and squares of Mayfair were appearing, while as early as 1688 Edward Shepherd had been granted a licence for his cattle market in Brookfield, a field just to the west of Devonshire House. Within a few years, permission was also given for the holding of the first May fair, in the market place, but it was not until the 1730s that the building of Berkeley Square, in its heyday the most fashionable and elegant of all the Mayfair squares, was under way.

Berkeley Square can be reached from Piccadilly via Berkeley

Berkeley Square.
Marianne Taylor

Street. A few of the houses have survived and the most beautiful of them all is Number 44, the small Palladian house designed by William Kent for Lady Isabella Finch, an unmarried daughter of the Earl of Winchilsea and Lady of the Bedchamber to Princess Amelia, sister of George II.

The Finches were a strange family, known as the 'black, funereal Finches', and Bel had inherited their swarthy skin and rather gloomy, melancholy temperament. Horace Walpole, who came to live on the other side of the square, wrote of a 'funeral loo' party he had attended at Bel Finch's, but the house, into which she moved in 1774, was outstanding.

From the outside it looks little different from the other eighteenth-century survivors in the square, and the small, square entrance hall is plain and simple, but passing through to the inner hall, one steps into the full beauty of the house. To the left is the small recess, where Bel's footmen sat to await their orders. To the right rises a magnificent staircase of Portland stone, with a balustrade of delicate ironwork. At the half landing it divides into two wide arcs, reaching the first floor past a screen of Ionic columns and continuing up to the minstrels' gallery and a gilded glass dome, which gives the hall a feeling of immense, soaring height.

The pride of the house is the grand salon on the first floor, stretching the entire width of the house and rising to a splendid painted ceiling.

In stately splendour, Bel Finch entertained, and the passage behind the Ionic screen is still known as Lady Bett's hiding place, for it was here that Bel's friend, Lady Betty Germaine, used to peep through and report to her which visitors were mounting that glorious staircase.

And presiding over the house and servants was her devoted major-domo, in his green livery and grey-powdered peruke.

When she died, in 1773, Lord Clermont bought the house and over the years it had several more owners. Not until 1959 did it pass out of private ownership and become the Clermont Club, but Bel Finch's major-domo, who loved the house so well, has lingered on to this day. Over the last two hundred years his ghost has been seen, still in his green livery and peruke, walking with a slight limp up and down the staircase, keeping a careful eye on things, watching the play of roulette and backgammon in the salon, and the footmen's alcove at the foot of the stairs, which is now the club bar, and then retiring silently through one of the staircase doors and up the narrow spiral staircase to his bedroom at the top of the house.

He is a benign and dignified ghost, well suited to Kent's masterpiece, which is now regarded as one of the six most architecturally important town houses in London.

The second haunted house of Berkeley Square is not next door, where Lord Clive committed suicide, but five houses away, at Number 50. For the first hundred years of its existence, from 1745, all was well, and one of its occupants was George Canning: but after the middle of the nineteenth century it fell empty for a few years, and like many an empty house, developed an air of gloom and mystery. Strange noises were heard coming from it. It could have been rats running among the bell ropes, or the wind moaning down the cold chimneys, but before long the conviction grew that something very strange was happening there and the place was haunted by malignant spirits. One resident of the square told of 'pandemonium sometimes breaking out in the house, Number 50, which was then empty . . .and always at night'.

190

One theory was that it was the ghost of an insane member of an aristocratic family who had once been kept there, a man so violent that he had to be locked up in an upper room and fed through a slot in the door, but this sounds too much like the story of Lord Chatham at Wildwood House or the haunted room at Glamis, where some member of the family, victim of a monstrous birth, had been kept in secrecy.

The description of the Berkeley Square ghost lost nothing in the telling and was described as a nameless horror – a man with grotesque and horrible features, white and flaccid cheeks bordering a gaping red mouth, or alternatively a creature with tentacles, that emerged from time to time from the London sewers.

The house was thought to be empty, yet about once every two months the sound of heavy furniture and boxes being moved over bare floors was heard. Sometimes bells were heard ringing, and once or twice curious people would enter the house, but saw nothing except the still swinging bells. Then there was a new development. A window would sometimes open and small objects – books, stones, pens and spurs – were hurled into the street. One morning the inhabitants of the square awoke to find that every window in the front of the house had been smashed.

Most were agreed that the trouble came from a front room on the second floor, and a young baronet said he would sleep there to see what would happen, promising to ring the bell twice, if he needed help. His friends waited below, and as midnight struck, they heard one pull on the bell, and immediately afterwards, a second, loud one. They rushed upstairs and found the young man sprawled across the bed, his head nearly touching the floor. There was a look of abject horror on his face and he was quite dead.

In 1872 Lord Lytton in *Notes and Queries* said it was quite true that the house in Berkeley Square was haunted and long unoccupied on that account. He had slept a night in the room, armed with two blunderbusses. Something had leaped towards him, and as he fired, it fell to the floor: but then it completely disappeared, so he was unable to say what it was.

There is also a sad story of a girl called Adeline, who lived there in the guardianship of a lecherous and wicked uncle. One day he tried to rape her, whereupon she threw herself out of the window and died.

In 1879 *Notes and Queries* published an excerpt from a periodical called *Mayfair*, which gave an even more detailed account of all the horrors connected with the house.

'The story of the haunted house in the heart of Mayfair is so far acquiesced in the silence of those who alone know the whole truth, and whose interest it is that the whole truth should be known. That story can be recapitulated in a few words. The house in Berkeley Square contains at least one room of which the atmosphere is supernaturally fatal to body and mind. A girl saw, heard, or felt such horror in it that she went mad, and never recovered sanity enough to tell how or why. A gentleman, a disbeliever in ghosts, dared to sleep in it, and was found a corpse in the middle of the floor after frantically ringing for help in vain. Rumour suggests other cases of the same kind, all ending in death, madness or both, as the result of sleeping, or trying to sleep in the room. The very party-walls of the house, when touched, are found saturated with electric horror. It is uninhabited save by an elderly man and woman who act as caretakers; but even these have no access to *the* room. This is kept locked, the key being in the hands of a mysterious and seemingly nameless person, who comes to the house once every six months, locks up the elderly couple in the basement, and then unlocks *the* room, and occupies himself in it for hours. Finally, and most wonderful of all, the house, though in Berkeley Square, is neither to be let nor sold. Its mere outside shows it to be given up to ghosts and decay.'

This story approximates to that told by Ralph Nevill, in his book *Romantic London*, for he was a relative of one of the families concerned in the mystery. From 1841 to 1859 the house was taken by the Honourable Elizabeth Curzon and then fell empty, developing its air of gloom and mystery.

Lady Mary Nevill married a Mr Myers, of whom her family did not approve, and for years the two families ignored each other. The time came, in the 1860s, when their son was engaged to be married, and Number 50, Berkeley Square was on the market at a bargain price. He had heard the stories of the maidservant who had slept in the haunted room and gone mad and the young baronet who had been found dead, but decided to ignore them all and set about preparing the house for his bride. He ordered furniture, carpets and china, and engaged two maidservants, but a few days before the wedding, the young woman jilted him and married someone else.

Poor young Myers was so shocked and heartbroken, that he never left the house again, and gradually went mad. For the next twenty years everything stayed as it was on the day he had received the news. The china and glass were still in their crates, the furniture unpacked and the carpets in rolls, as they had left the warehouse.

Coal and provisions were regularly delivered at the house, but the two servants seem to have become as silent and uncommunicative as their master: and as he never went outside the door, no one would believe that he was there at all. But at night time he would wander about the empty, dusty rooms, and the glint of his candle, which could sometimes be seen through the uncurtained windows, gave rise to the story that the house was being used by a gang of counterfeit coiners, who had broken in, through an underground passage from the mews, and established themselves in the basement.

The only contact he had with the outside world was an occasional visit from his sister, and when he died he left her everything, but the house remained empty until her death, growing each year more squalid and decayed, and it claimed yet another victim.

Two sailors, on Christmas leave in London, were looking for somewhere to spend the night. They saw the derelict house and broke into it. Soon they were asleep in one of the empty rooms, but suddenly they were awakened by a mysterious, menacing intruder. One of the sailors grabbed a curtain pole and prepared to fight off the creature, while the other dashed through the open door into the street. He ran into a policeman and begged him for help, but at that moment they heard a scream and the crash of breaking glass. The first sailor had flung himself through the window and came hurtling down on to the railings, where he was impaled. When they reached him, he was dead.

Despite this long story of sinister tragedies, in 1880 the Earl of Selkirk bought the house. He had it completely restored and redecorated, and from that time onwards no more was ever heard of the ghosts.

THE LEGEND OF THE KNIGHTS' BRIDGE

It is a pleasant walk of about a mile and a quarter to Kensington Palace, westwards down Piccadilly to Hyde Park Corner and then on, in the same direction, with Hyde Park and Kensington Gardens on your right, along Knightsbridge and the Kensington Road, as far as the Royal Garden Hotel, behind which you will see the palace.

The legend of Knightsbridge (7) belongs to the days of the Crusaders, when the West Bourne river, flowing from the heights of Hampstead, crossed this way and was spanned by a stone bridge, built, it is said, by Edward the Confessor, for the use of the monks of Westminster.

A party of knights, before embarking on their holy war, were making their way to the Bishop of London's palace at Fulham, for his blessing, but as they were crossing the bridge, two of them began to argue. The argument turned to a quarrel, and soon they were fighting. And while their companions watched from the banks of the stream, the two struggled on bitterly, until at last both fell into the water and were drowned.

THE GHOST OF KENSINGTON PALACE

Kensington Palace (8) developed from Nottingham House. The house was first built, early in the seventeenth century, by Sir George Coppins, but in 1620 he sold it to the dour Sir Heneage Finch, an ancestor of Bel Finch, who lived at 44 Berkeley Square. His son, another Sir Heneage, inherited it, and he and his son were even more melancholy than the first Sir Heneage, but the second became Lord Chancellor, and when he was made an Earl of Nottingham, the house in Kensington was called Nottingham House.

Kensington Palace.
British Tourist Authority

When William III came to England, he had no liking for the damp, decaying Whitehall Palace and spent most of his time at Hampton Court, which at one time he had a fancy for rebuilding as a second Versailles Palace, but the government disliked both the expense that would have been involved and the fact that the King would be so far from London, so King William compromised and bought Nottingham House from the Finches, for at the time it was unoccupied.

Here, after a good deal of extension and rebuilding, he and Queen Mary spent a good deal of their time. Queen Anne and Prince Frederick were fond of the palace and also the two first Georges, but the young George III 'desired to be excused living at Kensington' and eventually established Queen Charlotte and their large family at Buckingham Palace. For the next sixty years, no English monarch was to live at Kensington, but many members of the royal family were given apartments there, including George III's fifth daughter, the Princess Sophia, who was born in 1777.

In their childhood, the thirteen surviving children of the King and Queen spent much of their time at Windsor Castle or Kew Palace. Their régime was strict, formal and frugal, and Queen Charlotte, though she doted on the Prince of Wales, was a martinette where the rest of the family was concerned, and was particularly strict with the Princesses, even decreeing what clothes they should wear, which were invariably several years behind the current fashions. As for their marriages, she seemed to have no interest in them at all, and the King, who loved them dearly in his fashion, is said to have burst into tears if ever the subject were mentioned.

The unhappiest of the Princesses was Princess Sophia. In 1788, when she was only eleven years old, Thomas Garth was appointed a royal equerry. He was then forty-four, but from the first time they met, she was attracted to him. Soon she was deeply in love, and in 1799 she retired from Court for a while, suffering from an illness which was never explained. She was, in fact, having Garth's son, but the birth was kept a closely guarded secret. Even the King presumably knew nothing about it, for Garth remained at Court and was a particular favourite.

Princess Sophia returned to Court and the affair continued, though he was by no means attractive. In fact Greville later described him as a 'hideous old Devil, old enough to be her father and with a great claret mark on his face'.

With the passing years, however, Garth's ardour seems to have cooled, although from time to time the Princess saw her son.

The Queen died in 1818 and the King in 1820: and after this, the Princess was given apartments in Kensington Palace, on the first floor of the north-east corner of Clock Court. Her brother, the Duke of Sussex, was living in his own quarters, in the southern part of Clock Court, the Duchess of Kent and the baby Victoria in another part of the palace.

Young Garth visited the Princess at the palace, from time to time, and he joined the army, but never rose above the rank of Captain, for, according to Greville, he was 'an idiot as well as a rogue'.

General Garth died in 1829, 'a fine gentleman of the old school in powder and pigtail', according to one report, but in a book published anonymously, in 1832, *The Authentic Records of the Court of England for the last Seventy Years*, we read: 'In

November of this year (1829), died Thomas Garth, esquire, general in his Majesty's service, and colonel of the First or Royal regiment of Dragoons. This gallant general had the good fortune to render himself agreeable to a certain lady of illustrious birth, by whom, *it was said*, he had one son, who bears the general's name, and who now is captain in the army. The son was the chief mourner at the funeral of the general, which took place on the 27th of November, at St Martin's in the Fields. It is, however, very probable, that the mystery of this very extraordinary affair will, ere long, be explained, though it may not redound to the *chastity* of royalty. Many places and pensions have been bestowed to prevent the exposure of the circumstances attending the captain's birth, but we have reason to think that TRUTH will ultimately prevail. *We* could ourselves elucidate this matter a *little*, if we deemed it requisite. In referring to subjects of this nature, we cannot help pitying the imbecility and sorrows of George the Third, which were, doubtless, considerably heightened, though not originally produced, by the delinquencies of his family, both *male* and *female*.'

The author of this piece of malevolence was almost certainly the fervently Whig Lady Elizabeth Hamilton, a descendant of Lady Archibald Hamilton, who was a mistress of Frederick, Prince of Wales, George III's father.

After his father's death, Captain Garth tried to blackmail the royal family into giving him an annuity of £3,000 a year, in exchange for the documents he possessed, proving that he was the son of Princess Sophia, but by this time too many people knew about it and he was refused. He disappeared and was never heard of again, but the Princess Sophia stayed on at Kensington Palace.

The Duchess of Kent became involved with Sir John Conroy, and he was also controller to Princess Sophia, dominating her completely and, it would seem, getting his hands on much of her money, for when she died she had only £1,600 of her personal fortune left; but in 1837, when Victoria succeeded to the throne, she dismissed Conroy and moved to Buckingham Palace, her mother also being given rooms there, though as far away from the royal apartments as possible.

Princess Sophia was lonelier than ever, for the Duke of Sussex, who had been separated for years from his first wife, remarried after her death and seldom used his apartments in the Palace after that.

She was growing old and her eyesight was failing. As long as she could, she passed her lonely days at her spinning wheel or her embroidery frame, but in 1838 she became totally blind. She was moved to York House, close by, in Church Street, for her last few years, but her sad spirit still haunts Kensington Palace and the humming of her spinning wheel can still sometimes be heard in Clock Court.

THE GHOST OF HOLLAND HOUSE

From Kensington Palace, it is only a short walk westwards, past Kensington Church Street and along Kensington High Street, to Holland Park and the sad remains, after the bombing of World War Two, of Holland House (9). The east wing has been restored and incorporated in the new King George VI Memorial Youth Hostel, and enough of the frontage of the house has survived and been preserved to show how beautiful it once was – a fairy palace, with its oriel windows and Dutch gables, its arched colonnades and little stone towers, incongruously at variance with the adjacent Commonwealth Institute, with its split levels and open staircase, its blue glass and its copper covered roof, which looks like a vast Bedouin tent.

Holland House was built by Sir Walter Cope, early in the seventeenth century, soon after the accession of James I, and descended to his daughter, Isabella, wife of Sir Henry Rich, the handsome and elegant son of the Earl of Warwick, who became Lord Holland, and on whom both King James and his daughter-in-law, Henrietta Maria, doted.

Lord Holland, from being the impecunious 'younger son of a noble house, and a very fruitful bed', as Lord Clarendon neatly put it, became immensely rich and made many additions to Holland House, including the wings, the Long Gallery and the superbly decorated Gilt Room over the porch, which was designed for the ball the Hollands planned for the celebration of the marriage of Charles I and Henrietta Maria, but which, for no known reason, was not held.

Much of the work on the house was never paid for, but the Hollands prospered in royal favour until the outbreak of the Civil War. During the early months, when the struggle seemed to be favouring the King, Lord Holland was an ardent Royalist, serving as a General of the Horse, but by 1643, after the failure of his Scottish campaign, he, like many Royalists, had a change of heart.

His army was disbanded and he returned to Holland House. By August 1647, he was meeting there with General Fairfax and members of Parliament, to plan the last stages of the war, but when it suddenly became clear to him that the King's life was now in danger, he had second thoughts, remembering all the benefits he had received from him and the Queen.

He made an eleventh-hour attempt to change the course of events by enlisting the help of the young Duke of Buckingham and leading the insurrection at Kingston, but they were hopelessly outnumbered, and it proved an easy victory for Parliament.

Lord Holland was taken prisoner and kept at Warwick Castle for a time and then brought a prisoner to his own Holland House, from where he was brought for his trial. On March 9th, 1640, only a few weeks after the execution of King Charles, he suffered the same fate. Elegant to the last, 'the gay, beautiful, gallant Lord of Holland' made a long speech on the scaffold and then 'pulled off his gown and doublet, having next to him a white satin waistcoat, put on a white satin cap with silver lace and prepared himself for the block. . .prayed awhile, then gave the signal by stretching forth his arms, upon which the executioner severed his head from his body at one blow. . .'

Lady Holland fled into hiding in the country and General Fairfax moved into Holland House, where Cromwell and Ireton came often, to confer with him, but before long the house was restored to the widowed Lady Holland, who lived there until her death, with her eldest son Robert, and the ghost of his father for long afterwards haunted the beautiful gilt room. 'It issues forth at midnight from behind a secret door, and walks slowly through the scenes of his former triumphs, with his head in his hand', declared Aubrey, who had been told the story by a 'person of honour', who had presumably seen the ghost for himself. And not only did the Earl haunt the house, but his daughter, 'the beautiful Lady Diana Rich, as she was walking in her father's garden at Kensington, to take the fresh air before dinner, about eleven o'clock, being then very well, met with her own apparition, habit and everything, as in a looking glass. About a month after, she died of the smallpox. And it is said that her sister, the Lady Elizabeth Thynne, saw the like of herself before she died'.

JOSEPH ADDISON AND HOLLAND HOUSE

Robert, the second Earl of Holland, succeeded to the title of Earl of Warwick, and on his death his infant son Edward succeeded to both titles. During his childhood the house was let for a time, legend says to William Penn. Edward returned there on his marriage, but he died young, in 1701, leaving the widowed Charlotte, Countess of Warwick, with a small son: and it was Charlotte who took for her second husband, Joseph Addison, who had been in love with her for years and was, at that time, living at Sandford Manor, on the borders of Fulham and Chelsea, which had once been the reputed home of Nell Gwyn.

Addison moved into Holland House, but the marriage was said to have been unhappy. The gossips whispered that he would pace up and down the long library 'between two bottles of wine. . .taking a glass of each as he arrived at each end of the room' and to escape the lash of Charlotte's sharp tongue, spent hours in the White Horse Inn, at the bottom of Holland Lane.

But Addison was already a sick man, suffering from both dropsy and asthma, and less than three years later, in June, 1719, he died.

GEORGE III AND LADY SARAH LENNOX

The young Lord Warwick did not long survive Addison and

Remains of Holland House.
British Tourist Authority

Holland House was eventually bought by Henry Fox, the first Lord Holland of a new line. Much against her parents' wishes, Henry married the beautiful Lady Caroline Lennox, a great-granddaughter of Charles II and the Duchess of Portsmouth. They had other plans for her, but when she was told to prepare herself to meet the suitor of their choice, the story goes that she cut off her eyebrows and made herself look so odd, that they had to postpone the meeting: and that night she ran away and made a 'Fleet' marriage, at that time legal, at the chapel in the Fleet prison.

Her younger sister, Sarah, who was only fourteen, came to live with the Hollands, after the death of her parents, and attended George II's court at Kensington Palace. Here the future George III, still very young himself, fell in love with her, despite his attachment to Hannah Lightfoot, the Quakeress, whom many said he had married and was maintaining in Hampstead, with their two children.

This was after Hannah's hastily arranged marriage with Isaac Axford in 1753, at Keith's Chapel in Curzon Street, which was never consummated, since she was abducted at the Chapel door by the mysterious occupant of a coach and never seen or heard of again by her family or Axford.

When he came to the throne, George III's love for Sarah was greater than ever and Hannah seems to have been forgotten, although the story goes that she died young and was buried under an assumed name.

Henry Fox was more than interested in the prospect of becoming the brother-in-law of the Queen of England, and, according to Horace Walpole, in the summer of 1761, although Fox 'went himself to bathe in the sea (possibly to disguise his intrigue), he left Lady Sarah at Holland House, where she appeared every morning in a field close to the great road (where the King passed on horseback) in a fancied habit, making hay'.

The affair went no further, for the Queen Mother, too, sensed what was afoot, and forthwith sent her ambassador to Hanover, to arrange young George's marriage with someone of her own choice, the seventeen-year-old Charlotte of Mecklenburg-Strelitz: and so complete was the King's deference to the will of his mother, said Walpole, that he blindly accepted the bride she had chosen for him; though to the very day of the council, he carried on his courtship of Lady Sarah.

So poor Sarah, instead of being a royal bride, was one of Queen Charlotte's ten bridesmaids, but people said that during the marriage ceremony, King George had eyes only for Lady Sarah instead of for Charlotte.

THE LAST YEARS OF HOLLAND HOUSE

It was during the late eighteenth century and the early years of the nineteenth century, when the third Lord Holland was living at Holland House, that it became famous as the centre of Whig society, entertaining the Royal Dukes as well as men of letters, including Lord Byron: and it was here that Lady Caroline Lamb met him and pursued their strange, capricious love affair.

After Lord Holland's death his son carried on the tradition, but the house was becoming increasingly expensive to maintain, and after his death, his widow had to sell parts of the estate and hand over its management to her heir, the fifth Earl of Ilchester. Lady Holland died in 1889, and while rural Kensington disappeared in ever more building, Lord and Lady Ilchester maintained the house with loving care and preserved the 'cuckoo haunted wilderness' of the remaining grounds. The last grand function was held there in July, 1939, a ball which King George VI and Queen Elizabeth attended, but then came World War Two and the bombs which destroyed it.

FROM VICTORIA STATION TO CHELSEA

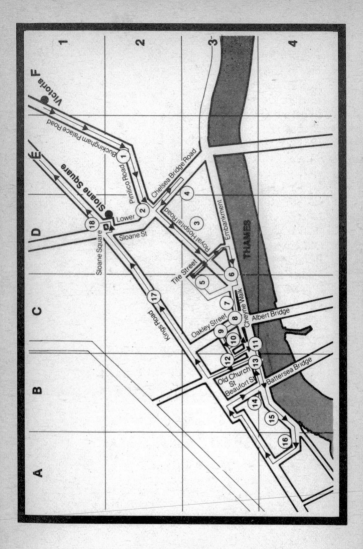

J

J

BUSES
Buckingham Palace Road/Pimlico Road: 11, 39.
Victoria Station: 10, 16, 16A, 25, 38, 39, 52, 149, 500, 507.
Royal Hospital Road/Cheyne Walk: 39.
King's Road: 11, 19, 22, 49.
Sloane Square: 11, 19, 22, 137.

This is only a rough guide to the buses and you may need to consult the London Transport Bus Map.

UNDERGROUNDS
Victoria
Sloane Square

THE CHELSEA BUN HOUSE

From Victoria Station, turn left to the Grosvenor Hotel and then left again, down the Buckingham Palace Road, past Airways House, with the Victoria Coach Station on the opposite side of the road. Then take the right-hand fork – the Pimlico Road (1). At the far end,* from which run the Chelsea Bridge Road to the left and the Royal Hospital Road straight ahead, once stood the famous Chelsea Bun House (2).

It was established late in the seventeenth century, close to the gardens of Ranelagh House. It was a fair-sized, corner house, and on one side a colonnade was built over the pavement, in the shelter of which you could buy your buns at an open window, while inside was a room exhibiting all manner of curios, after the manner of Don Saltero's coffee house close by.

The buns were made from eggs, butter, sugar, lemon and spices, and there were said to be none like them anywhere else in London. They were enormously popular, and for a century or more the Bun House was high fashion. George II and Queen Caroline often called there, with the Princesses, and George III and Queen Charlotte took their children there on several occasions.

Living close by, at this time, was Mary Darby, who was to become the matchless Perdita, a mistress of the Prince of Wales. She was a few years older than the Prince, boarding at the alcoholic Mrs Lorrington's Seminary for Young Ladies in Church Lane (now Old Church Street), and she recalled the time when, no more than twelve years old, she had been taken to the Bun House, as a special treat, and caught her first glimpse of the handsome little Prince, who was to cause such havoc in her life a few years later, after her disastrous marriage to Thomas Robinson.

For four generations, the Bun House was run by the Hands family, to whom Nell Gwyn's mother, Mary Gwyn, claimed a relationship. She lived close by, in a cottage which had a little garden sloping down to the river, and one day, when she was allegedly very drunk, she fell into the water and was drowned.

*About a mile from Victoria Station.

THE ROYAL HOSPITAL AND NELL GWYN

The Chelsea Bridge Road and the Royal Hospital Road enclose the gardens of the Chelsea Hospital for Wounded and Superannuated Soldiers (**3**). For years there was a legend that Nell Gwynn had urged King Charles to found the hospital, after her heart had been wrung by the story of a crippled soldier, who had stopped her coach and asked her for alms. He told her that he had been wounded during the Civil War, fighting for the Stuart cause, whereupon she hurried to the King, told him of the old man's misery, and begged him to do something for the old soldiers who had suffered for him and been so cruelly neglected.

This story was believed for many years, and old soldiers at the hospital used to toast her memory and bless her as their benefactress, although it is also recorded that, in the early days, the inmates had no great liking for life in the hospital, with its strict regimen, and would have preferred a pension on which they could have lived independently. However, they soon settled down contentedly, and near the hospital was a Nell Gwynn tavern which bore an inscription on its signboard bearing testimony to her kindness. As late as 1795, when Daniel Lysons published his *Environs of London*, he mentioned the story, although he doubted its truth. It is a myth which has died very hard, but there is no record of Nell ever having had anything to do with the founding of the hospital.

Only a few months after his Restoration, King Charles had promised to look after the soldiers who had fought for him during the troubles at Tangiers. 'They shall always be my particular care and protection', he had said, but for the first few years of his reign, he was prevented by lack of funds. Not only did the Treasury have to contend with the disasters of the Plague and the Great Fire, but there was strong resistance from the Opposition, who disapproved of the King's army – the Grenadier, Coldstream and Royal Horse Guards – and at one time even declared it illegal.

In 1670, Louis XIV founded the *Hôtel Royal des Invalides* in Paris, and ten years later, the Duke of Ormonde established a similar military hospital near Dublin. Once more the question arose of a hospital for English soldiers. It was the army pay-

Founder's Day, Royal Hospital Chelsea.
British Tourist Authority

master, the immensely wealthy and humane Sir Stephen Fox, who made the first definite proposal, consulting first with John Evelyn, who was also anxious for the hospital to be established.

On the site eventually chosen for the hospital stood the theological college established by James I, to confute the doctrines of the Church of Rome and defend 'the true religion now established within the realm of England'. There was never enough money to complete it, and although it functioned, in a half-hearted way, for a few years, by the time of the Commonwealth the building was being used to house Scottish prisoners.

At the Restoration, an enthusiastic Anglican besought the King to re-establish the College, which had become 'a cage of unclean beasts, a stable for horses, and a resort of loose women', but Charles was not interested, and by 1665 the place was housing Dutch prisoners, John Evelyn being one of the four commissioners appointed to watch over their welfare.

At the end of the Dutch war, King Charles offered the building to the Royal Society, but it was so dilapidated by this time, that it proved of no use to them, and after the roof collapsed, Sir Christopher Wren, their President, could only advise its demolition.

211

Although the building was worthless, the land was valuable, and it was now that, with the help of Sir Stephen Fox, King Charles bought back the college. Wren made his plans and the building of the hospital began. Money was still short, for although the King and Sir Stephen both contributed generously, the Treasury gave nothing and a public fund had to be raised.

King Charles died before the building was completed but James II contributed and provided pensions for the men who had suffered for him during the Monmouth rebellion, it being arranged that these pensions should be paid to them until the hospital was ready to receive them.

LORD RANELAGH AND RANELAGH HOUSE

Lord Ranelagh had become Paymaster General, 'a young man of great parts and great vices'. He was appointed to supervise the completion of the hospital building, but at the same time he took an even greater interest in the building of his own Ranelagh House in the hospital grounds. By 1689 the Royal Hospital was nearly ready for occupation, but Lord Ranelagh managed to prolong proceedings for the next two and a half years, during which time he completed his own beautiful house and garden (4), to his own satisfaction and at the hospital's expense.

A Royal Commission transferred the management of the hospital to a committee of three, which included Sir Stephen Fox, Sir Christopher Wren and himself. Ranelagh could delay no longer, and in March, 1692, the hospital was opened. Five hundred pensioners were admitted during the first year, with more than a hundred living close by, as out-pensioners, all of them men who had proved that they had done good service 'by flood and field'. But the unfortunate out-pensioners were not paid their pensions, and 'lived in a miserable way upon credit in shops and lodging houses'. Lord Ranelagh came under suspicion, and in 1702, with debts amounting to £72,000, was accused of fraud and forced to resign. Yet he managed to persuade the Treasury Board that Ranelagh House was his own property, together with the ground he had appropriated, which amounted to nearly one-third of the land acquired for the hospital. A few years later he died, in poverty and ignominy, but his daughter, Lady Jones, was allowed to live on in the house, and was even granted a small pension.

By this time Queen Anne was on the throne, and after a closer watch was kept on the affairs of the hospital, the old abuses disappeared and it became a true and happy haven.

To this day, the pensioners wear the uniforms that their ancestors wore during the campaigns of the Duke of Marlborough – scarlet frock coats in summer and dark blue overcoats in winter, with three-cornered hats for special occasions, such as Oak Apple day, the 29th May, which celebrates the birthday of their founder, Charles II.

DR MESSENGER MONSEY

Dr Messenger Monsey was appointed physician to the hospital and lived in part of the old College, before it was finally demolished. He was a man of wit and erudition who became a legend in his own lifetime. Faulkner, in his *History of Chelsea*, writes that 'He lived so long in his office of Physician to the Chelsea Hospital, that, during many changes of administration, the reversion of his place had been successively promised to several medical friends of the Paymaster-General of the Forces. Looking out of his window one day, and observing a gentleman below examining the college and gardens, who he knew had secured the reversion of his place, the doctor came downstairs, and going out to him, accosted him thus: – "Well, sir, I see you are examining your house and gardens, that *are to be*, and I will assure you that they are both very pleasant and very convenient. But I must tell you one circumstance: you are the fifth man that has had the reversion of the place, and I have buried them all. And what is more," continued he, looking very scientifically at him, "there is something in your face that tells me I shall bury you too." The event justified the prediction, for the gentleman died some years after; and what is more extraordinary, at the time of the doctor's death there was not a person who seems to have even solicited the promise of the reversion.'

When the old doctor died at last, at the age of ninety-five, a large box was found in his rooms, full of air holes and fitted with poles, like a sedan chair. In this he wished to be carried to his friend, Mr Forster, 'in case he should be in a trance when supposed to be dead'.

He also left instructions that he should not be buried with any funeral ceremony, but be dissected and then thrown into the Thames, or wherever the surgeon who operated might please.

Dr Monsey lived through many changes in this part of Chelsea and saw the end of Ranelagh House. One of the last great events there was when Lady Jones was visited by George I, on the occasion of a great water pageant, for which Handel had composed his Water Music, conducting it himself from one of the barges, for the orchestra of fifty players, drifting up-river in the flotilla.

RANELAGH PLEASURE GARDENS

Not until 1733 was Ranelagh House put up for auction, and then it was bought, along with part of the gardens, by Lacy, a joint patentee with David Garrick of Drury Lane Theatre, and converted into the Ranelagh pleasure gardens (4). Soon they were successfully rivalling the older established Vauxhall Gardens, and Ranelagh remained fashionable until the end of the century: but gradually they lost their popularity, the standard of entertainment declined, and in 1805 the gardens were closed. The rotunda and Ranelagh House were demolished, and the gardens, with their Temple of Pan, the Venetian Temple and the ornamental canal were all dismantled and soon forgotten.

The Cremorne Gardens, less than a mile away, at the western end of Cheyne Walk, about where Cremorne Road (16) now runs, were opened during the 1840s, but they never attained the fashion and distinction of Ranelagh in its heyday. From the beginning, they were raffish and noisy, and about 1875 they were closed.

Although Nell Gwyn had no hand in the founding of the

Royal Hospital, she had a connection with Chelsea, apart from the Hands family of the Bun House, for she was said to have lived at Sandford Manor, which was at the western end of the village, on the Fulham border, and close to the World's End tavern and tea gardens in the King's Road. This was a highly popular, if somewhat disreputable resort in the time of Charles II, when the King's Road (17) was first made, as a private road for the King, to make the journey to Hampton Court, from Whitehall or St James's, easier and quicker. It was the house where, a few years later, Joseph Addison was to live before his marriage, but in the nineteenth century the old house was swallowed up in the buildings of the Imperial Gas Company.

Walk on westwards down Royal Hospital Road until you reach Tite Street (5) (see page 218). If you turn left at Tite Street you will reach the Chelsea Embankment. Continue westwards along the Embankment, passing the Physic Garden (6) on your right (see page 216) and into Cheyne Walk.

SIR THOMAS MORE

Until the early sixteenth century, Chelsea was no more than a handful of cottages clustered round the church and manor house, by the side of the marshy banks of the Thames. The first notable resident was Sir Thomas More, who built his house by the riverside, about where Beaufort Street (14) now runs: and it was from here that 'with a heavy heart, as by his countenance appeared, he took boat with his son Roper', for his trial and execution.

Many illustrious men had visited that Chelsea household, including the Bishop of Rochester, who was also to die for his convictions, Linacre, Thomas Heywood and Hans Holbein, who lived with the Mores for two or three years.

CHELSEA PALACE

After Sir Thomas More's death, King Henry gave his house to the Marquis of Winchester and set about building a palace for himself less than a quarter of a mile away, where Oakley Street **(8)** now lies: and here the Princess Elizabeth and little Prince Edward spent the years of their childhood.

Like Sir Thomas More's house, which had been rebuilt and named Beaufort House, the royal palace survived into the eighteenth century.

THE CHEYNE FAMILY AND THE PHYSIC GARDEN

By the end of the sixteenth century there was a great revival of interest in agriculture and horticulture throughout the country and many new plants were introduced and cultivated. Market gardens were established in the London suburbs, to supply the growing needs of the city, and those in Chelsea were particularly

Cheyne Walk, Chelsea.
British Tourist Authority

prosperous. It was after the Civil War that the Cheyne family became associated with Chelsea, for Lady Cheyne was the daughter of the Duke of Newcastle, and after he returned from exile in Holland, and the family recovered their fortune, she and her husband, Charles Cheyne, were able to buy the manor and palace of Chelsea. Lord Cheyne was a keen gardener and he leased a plot of land of between three and four acres, just to the west of where the Royal Hospital was to be built, to the Society of Apothecaries, for the creation of a 'Botanical or Physic Garden' (**6**).

If you walk westwards along the Chelsea Embankment, from the Chelsea Bridge Road, you will find it still, and Sir Hans Sloane comes into the story again, for not only had he succeeded brilliantly in his profession and become a baronet, but by marrying a rich wife had become very wealthy. He bought the manor of Chelsea from the Cheyne family and granted the freehold of the Physic Garden to the Society of Apothecaries. Here, in 1722, Philip Miller was appointed director, a post which he held for the next fifty years, during which he compiled his splendid *Dictionary of Gardening.* And today the Physic Garden is known to botanists all over the world, for its unrivalled collection of plants, for its research into problems of plant biology and for its valuable teaching facilities.

Having dispelled the illusion of Nell Gwyn's connection with the Royal Hospital, there are no more legends in Chelsea which are not based on history, a history so colourful that a riverside walk down Cheyne Walk is a happy excursion into the past. Number 18 is the site of Don Saltero's coffee-house. As plain John Salter he had been a servant of Sir Hans Sloane and accompanied him on his travels, during which he, too, acquired a taste for collecting. He called himself a gimcrack-whim collector, and displayed in his coffee-house such assorted trivia as a piece of Solomon's Temple, the Pope's infallible candle, Mary Queen of Scots' pincushion, manna from Canaan, a starved swallow, the head of an Egyptian, the Emperor of Morocco's tobacco pipe, a curious flea trap and the jaws of a wild boar that was starved to death by its tusks growing inward, all carefully arranged in glass cases, in the room above the shop, and visited by hundreds of people, including such men as Richard Cromwell, the former Protector, Sir Richard Steele and Benjamin Franklin.

Defoe had called Chelsea a town of palaces, but by the eighteenth century the palaces were fast disappearing and in their place the first riverside houses of Cheyne Walk were built and the delightful smaller houses in the terraces behind, many of which have survived.

Writers and artists came to live there – Addison at Sandford Manor, Steele in Cheyne Walk. Swift lodged in Old Church Street. Sir Robert Walpole's house was close to the Royal Hospital. At the Queen's House in Cheyne Walk lived Dante Gabriel Rossetti. Thomas and Jane Carlyle were for years in Cheyne Row, and their house has been preserved for the public to visit. Leigh Hunt lived round the corner, in Upper Cheyne Row.

At Number 119, a small cottage at the western end of Cheyne Walk (15), J M W Turner used often to come, from his house in Queen Anne Street and in a strange anonymity, calling himself Puggy Booth, he would spend hours on the little balcony he had built for himself on the roof. Here, wrapped in a thick dressing gown, he sat watching the endlessly changing pattern of the dawn and sunset skies and the 'ever-moving clouds and river'.

It was in this cottage that he died, in December, 1851. It was a grey, dreary day, but it was said that, in his last hour, 'the sun burst forth and shone directly on him, with that brilliancy which he loved to gaze on'.

In Tite Street (5), which runs from the Embankment north-westwards, across the Royal Hospital Road, James Whistler built the White House for himself, although, after only a few months, he was declared bankrupt and had to leave it, moving to Number 13. Oscar Wilde was living with his wife and two small sons at Number 16, at the time of his arrest and downfall. John Sargent lived at Number 31.

The site of the little Chelsea porcelain works was at the corner of Justice Walk (12) and Lawrence Street (11), and it opened in the 1740s. In its heyday, under the management of Nicholas Sprimont, it employed at least a hundred people, both men and women, and a contemporary writer observed that 'this propinquity proved very injurious to their morals'.

After Sprimont's death, in the 1770s, William Duesbury carried on for a time, in a small way, but in 1783 he moved the works to Derby.

The Chelsea factory was demolished and the present small houses built on the site, but the little Chelsea porcelain figures, the fishermen and gardeners, the flower sellers and beggars, the wandering musicians, the watermen and the masqueraders from Ranelagh all recall the everyday life of the beautiful riverside village during the eighteenth century.

The most interesting way back to Victoria Station is to walk up Old Church Street (13) to the King's Road (17) and then turn right, back to Sloan Square Station (18), which is only one station away from Victoria, on the District or Circle line.

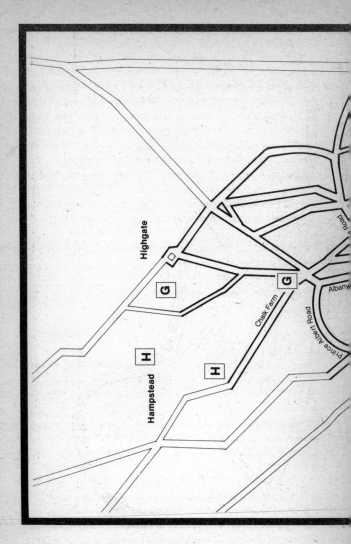

The Key to Reference Map starts on page 222

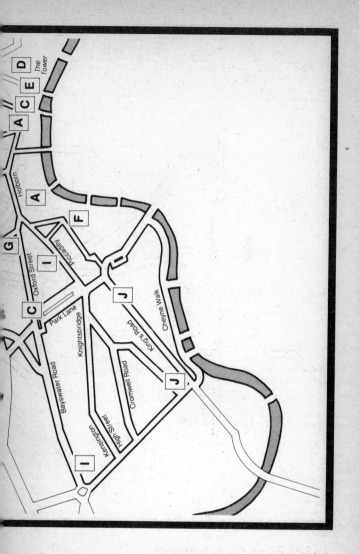

KEY TO REFERENCE MAP